ESP: A PERSONAL
MEMOIR

ESP: A PERSONAL MEMOIR

BY ROSALIND HEYWOOD

With an Introduction by Sir Cyril Burt, D.Sc., F.B.A.

Professor Emeritus of Psychology in the University of London

NEW YORK

E. P. DUTTON & CO., INC.

CONTENTS

PART I
GENERAL BACKGROUND

PART II
PERSONAL BACKGROUND

PART III
PERSONAL EXPERIENCES

6 CONTENTS

Wee know the receipt, the capacity of the ventricle, the stomach of man, how much it can hold; and wee know the receipt of all the receptacles of blood, how much blood the body can have; so wee do of all the other conduits and cisterns of the body; But this infinite Hive of honey, this insatiable whirlpoole of the covetous mind, no Anatomy, no dissection hath discovered to us. . . .

John Donne, SERMON LXX

I must begin with a good body of facts and not from principle, in which I always suspect some fallacy. . . .

Charles Darwin

ESP: A PERSONAL MEMOIR

INTRODUCTION

'The richest field for new discoveries,' wrote William James to his brother Henry, 'is the odd, unclassified residuum.' Round the rim of each of those neat and orderly systems we call science there lurks a handful of queer and unaccountable phenomena, often trifling in themselves, which, when dragged into the open and scrutinized more closely, have furnished the starting points of entirely new conceptions. The most striking instances are those out-of-the-way anomalies of nineteenth century physics—black-body radiations, the photo-electric effect, and the arrangement of lines in the spectrum of hydrogen—oddities which, when systematically re-investigated during the early years of the present century, gave rise to the quantum theory, and so revolutionized the whole basis of modern science. There are similar unexplained peculiarities in the field of human behaviour. The strange occurrences, reported from time to time, which suggest the influence of such problematic processes as telepathy, clairvoyance, and precognition, form the most baffling elements in the 'unclassified residuum' left on one side in the academic study of the mind.

Psychology is itself a science; and the sciences, it is popularly supposed, are progressively built up by a succession of deliberate experiments and observations carried out by a team of specialists in pursuance of a preconceived scheme. But that is only part of a long and intricate story. Too often we forget how much we owe in every branch of science to the inquiring amateur, to the shrewd observer of common things or uncommon incidents—in short, to the snapper-up of unconsidered trifles.

It is as in interested amateur that Mrs Heywood depicts herself in the following pages. In all humility she modestly disclaims any pretension to being regarded as a scientist by training. Many of her readers, versed in the more rigorous and older branches of physical science, may accordingly be tempted to dismiss some of the observations she here reports as too commonplace to be worth attention, or too fanciful to be studied seriously by the hard headed critic in a technological age. Yet, as those who have read her earlier volume, *The Sixth Sense*, will readily testify, she is equipped with a highly critical mind, and is fully alive to snags and pitfalls that beset her subject. Nor does she fail to appreciate the value of experimental techniques and the need for statistical checks.

Unfortunately in the field of 'parapsychology' (to borrow the current term) it has proved peculiarly difficult to devise tests and experiments which shall be at once fool-proof and fraud-proof, nor is it easy to hit on methods of investigation which will disclose the hidden processes and complex causative factors that are actually at work. Hitherto the only procedures which have furnished positive and trustworthy data have necessitated such strict and artificial conditions that the results obtained seem to have little bearing on the practical problems of daily life. The simple fact that a few exceptional persons are at times able to guess the numbers or the pictures on specially constructed cards rather more frequently than a statistician would expect from sheer chance is in itself a discovery of very slender interest. And yet, once we have demonstrated that something like 'extra-sensory perception' does in fact occur, if only in the rather trivial instances that lend themselves to laboratory checks, it becomes plausible to consider its possibility in the far more illuminating cases of apparent telepathy, clairvoyance, or precognition, which seem to occur in the lives of certain individuals, more or less spontaneously, as they go about their ordinary business.

Some of the examples that Mrs Heywood reports are of the familiar type met with in the published accounts that report the observations of professional 'mediums' and 'sensitives'; and, coming as they do from an exceptionally cautious and critical witness whose integrity is beyond all question, they supply a much-needed confirmation. But her book includes at least two special kinds of experience which to my mind are comparatively new in the literature of the subject, and deserve the attention of the professional psychologist. The first is what she calls the 'Singing'—apparently a quasi-musical experience, resembling that which one hears on cupping a hand over the ear-hole and varying the concavity of the palm, or that of Wordsworth's

> Curious child, applying to his ear
> The convolutions of a smooth-lipped shell,
> To which, in silence hushed, his very soul
> Listened intensely; for from within were heard
> Murmurings, whereby the monitor expressed
> Mysterious union with its native sea:
> Even such a shell the universe itself is.

With Mrs Heywood the sound is not localized within the ear itself, nor yet in any one specific direction, but is apparently 'spread out all round'. And to her it seems to express (as it did to myth makers and the poets of old) the inner nature of the environment at the moment, whether mountain or moor, church or ancient library. To a couple of friends who related similar experiences (one of them an eminent scholar of world wide reputation) it appeared at 'a moment of revelation'. A couple of suggestive characteristics may be noted. First, when another person happens to have heard the 'singing' in the same place at the same time, the sounds apparently possess the same general character for both the hearers. Secondly, they are, or at least they may be, informative; and the information, we are told, has in some instances been duly checked. On other occasions 'it does not convey anything *specific*, but is only a kind of background atmosphere', which, we are told, would be difficult to define in words.

The other set of experiences she calls receiving 'Orders'. An authoritative instruction, or at least an authoritative urge, suddenly comes to her, bidding her undertake some seemingly unreasonable mission, which, as the event disclosed, had useful or important consequences. The 'Singing' would probably be classed by the orthodox psychologist as a passing 'hallucination'—a convenient technical term which to him would not necessarily imply that the experiences were pathological, and merely designates a sensory impression which arises without any corresponding physical stimulation of the sense organ. The 'Orders' seem to belong to a less familiar class of experiences for which the English language has no appropriate name. Mrs Heywood explains that they are devoid of specific sensory content—like a mental 'voice' or an imaginary 'vision', but are more like 'hunches' and 'urges': 'I *felt* (she says) as though someone was telling me . . .' Experiences of this type are surely of supreme importance for parapsychology, although they are seldom explicitly recognized. Long ago, during the early years of the present century, the German school of introspective psychology, by dint of laboratory experiments carried out with trained observers, succeeded in establishing a group—or rather several groups—of elusive experiences which are neither actual sensations nor copies of sensations: some they termed 'imageless thoughts'; others 'determining tendencies'; and others again '*Gestaltqualitäten*', i.e. shape-like qualities (e.g., the 'grin without the cat'). All were characterized by the fact that they were, in the German phrase, *unanschaulich* ('impalpable' is perhaps the nearest English equivalent). Mrs Heywood's experiences seem clearly to belong to this category.

It is, however, impossible to draw any sharp line between the half-unconscious semi-obsessive notions or impulses that we all of us experience and the downright hallucinations and compulsive actions of those who are admittedly abnormal. One of the earliest inquiries into these borderline experiences was that undertaken nearly eighty years ago by Sir Francis Galton. He noted, what numerous investigators have since confirmed, that occurrences of this kind are far commoner among sane and healthy persons than is generally realized. Those who experience them, he says, are apt to imagine that there must be some morbid cause. This is a lurking dread most psychologists encounter when making such investigations. Tactfully approached, something like one in three of the people I have questioned will end by confessing that they have had anomalous experiences of this kind, but have hitherto hesitated to mention them for fear their friends would regard them as either superstitious cranks or unbalanced neurotics —or perhaps a bit of both. The result is that psychological investigators, who seek to study every out-of-the-way type of mental phenomenon, find themselves extremely short of data in this particular field. Let us hope that Mrs Heywood's courage in confiding some of her intimate secrets to print will embolden others to do the same.

Taken at their face value, many of the singular episodes here recorded may seem at first sight to imply methods of communicating or acquiring knowledge which are, to say the least, mysterious or occult. King James I would have had no doubt as to where those 'Orders' came from; and his view could have been fully supported by showing that many of Mrs Heywood's gifts tally almost exactly with those set forth in His Majesty's *Demonology*. Had she lived in the seventeenth or eighteenth century, her fate would have been that of Agnes Sampson, or Elizabeth Style, or of an ancestress of her own, who (she says) was actually 'the last witch burnt in Scotland'. Today the chief line of criticism will probably be that science and common sense alike assure us that feats of this kind, though frequent enough in fiction and folklore, are beyond the bounds of serious credibility: that they are in fact impossibilities.

But, as every schoolgirl knows, the White Queen considered it part of her mental training to believe half-a-dozen impossible things every morning before breakfast; and the conscientious psychologist finds himself forced to credit a far larger number than that. Judged by the criteria of common sense and what the man on the bus calls science, it would be plainly impossible that the three pounds of putty-like substance which makes up the brain should mediate something so astonishing as actual consciousness, or that, when a patient's cerebral hemispheres have been divided in two by the surgeon's knife (as has sometimes proved necessary in certain rare disorders), he should still possess only a single consciousness. If we admit (as of course we must) that the miracle of ordinary *sense* perception is an undeniable fact of every day life, then what is termed *extra-sensory* perception becomes a comparatively minor exploit. It is unusual; it refuses to fit in with our present-day assumptions; but that is all.

However, I am inclined to think the names currently employed —'extra-sensory', 'para-normal', 'clair-voyant', 'psycho-kinetic', and the like—tend rather to increase than to allay the critic's incredulity. Convenient though it may be, the word 'extra-sensory' is one which Mrs Heywood herself, so she tells us, would prefer to avoid. And applied to her own experiences it is certainly at times something of a misnomer. To begin with, it suggests a classification of perceptions into two sharply contrasted types—the 'sensory' or normal, and the 'extra-sensory' or abnormal; whereas in point of fact much, if not most, of what passes for purely 'sensory' perception contains a large amount of extra-sensory material—interpretations that we read into our 'sensations', glosses that we unconsciously impose on them; and much of what is dubbed 'extra-sensory' perception is not a process of perception at all, but, as we have just seen, very often a rather obscure method of experiencing 'thoughts', 'ideas', or 'hunches'. Thus the question whether these elusive apprehensions are sensory or extra-sensory, becomes comparatively unimportant.

The alternative term, 'paranormal' (which Mrs Heywood herself avoids), may be even more misleading. When in the end we come to understand such cases as are genuinely veridical, we shall, I suspect, discover that the underlying processes are after all entirely normal, though by then, no doubt, our notions of normality will be greatly enlarged. In the early stage of the Society for Psychical Research 'mesmerism' was included among the main groups of 'paranormal' phenomena. Though consistently pooh-poohed by the physicians of the day, it was nevertheless considered to be well worth systematic study. Those investigations have since borne fruit. Today hypnotism is accepted by every doctor as perfectly normal, although it still remains no less mysterious than the nightly process of dropping off to sleep. So, I imagine, it will turn out with whatever else is ultimately established in this curious field.

The hypothetical frontier which divides the realm of apparent impossibilities from the hum-drum world of the apparently possible is continually shifting. What yesterday's scientists held to be incredible often forms an essential element in tomorrow's orthodoxy. The commonest type of criticism which the so-called parapsychologist has had to face takes its stand on what are sometimes called 'the basic limiting principles of science'. As these are commonly formulated, the 'normal,' and the 'paranormal' are defined in terms of what is traditionally known as 'mechanistic monism'.

The world-picture which in our schooldays most science masters presented to their classes conceived the universe as one gigantic machine—a vast deterministic system made up of indivisible and indestructible atoms of matter, moving about at varying speeds in absolute space and time, and in their motions obeying, with strict precision, certain extremely simple but inviolable laws, usually expressed as equations of motion. This was the universe of nineteenth century science. It was the universe of Pavlov and Watson, the founders of twentieth century behaviourism; it was the universe of Freud, the founder of psychoanalysis, though for descriptive purposes he allowed himself certain concessions; and it is the universe of those present-day psychologists who accept the prevailing behaviourist view—of Dr McLeish, for instance, whose *Science of Behaviour* appeared last year and is based on an emphatic rejection of the concepts of 'mind' and 'consciousness', and of Dr Hansel who is perhaps the best known of contemporary critics of parapsychology. 'All such ideas as clairvoyance, telepathy, and precognition', we are assured, 'can be definitely discarded in advance as utterly inconsistent with the basic principles of science, and therefore beyond the bounds of possibility'.

But this world-picture, adequate though it may be for certain limited purposes, is nevertheless quite incompatible with many other notions which quantum physicists of the present day readily accept as working hypotheses and often as established facts. The notion that matter, so far from being conserved, can be not only destroyed but continuously created, that the atom itself can be split, that its units can be conceived either as 'particles' or as 'waves', that indeterminacy is more fundamental than determinism, and that there are forces within the atom far more powerful than those of gravity, electricity, or magnetism—all this would have been rejected by the orthodox scientist of the nineteenth century, not merely as 'paranormal', but as 'beyond the bounds of possibility'. No doubt, if the processes within the brain obeyed the laws of classical or 'macroscopic' physics (as until recently most physiologists have tacitly assumed), we must be compelled to endorse the criticisms advanced by the behaviouristic school. But if, as now seems increasingly probable, such processes conform rather to the principles of subatomic or 'quantum' physics, then both psychical and parapsychical hypotheses can no longer be so abruptly ruled out.

The cosmos of present-day physics is not so much a universe as a multiverse. Interacting with the universe of Newtonian dynamics—and yet almost wholly unsuspected until a century or two ago—there is the universe of electromagnetic forces, no longer (as my schoolmaster believed and hoped) reducible to mechanical strains and stresses arising within the 'ether'. Side by side with the universe of 'particles' there is also the universe of 'fields'. These various 'universes' are not put forward as final pictures of the world; they are merely very imperfect and tentative 'thought-models', enabling us to interpret certain limited *aspects* of the wider whole. There is therefore no *a priori* reason why we should reject the idea of yet another universe of psychic forces or phenomena, interacting with the so-called material or physical universe. Whether there actually is such a universe is a matter for further empirical research.

This, however, is a highly complex problem which can only be approached by gradual steps; and the first of these must consist in the dull and down-to-earth business of discovering the exact nature of the mental processes involved. In the popular mind the central question is the question of validity—whether, for example, such intimations are genuinely veridical and whether they spring from some transcendental source. With this the present-day psychologist, as a mere scientist, is but little concerned. His provisional opinion, if he has one, must depend rather on his philosophical assumptions, his own personal experiences, or simply on the faith by which he lives (and there are many kinds of faith besides those that are primarily religious or theological). Before venturing to propound any scientific answer, he wants first of all to ascertain the humbler facts.

And it is here that Mrs Heywood's book has its chief value. She is one of the few observers who take special pains to analyse the detailed characteristics both of the experiences themselves and of the mental activities that seemed to underlie or initiate them. But at this point, like every other investigator who tries to break fresh ground, she finds herself handicapped by the lack of suitable repertory of concepts and clearly-defined terms to describe and analyse what is new and strange. Psychology suffers more than any other science because it is the only branch of knowledge that deals with states of consciousness as such. That is why so many modern psychologists have been attracted by behaviourism; overt behaviour can always be described in the ready-made language of everyday life, supplemented here and there by a few familiar concepts taken from the elementary physics and physiology of our schooldays.

The sensory equipment of the ordinary human being and the vocabulary that goes with it have been evolved, not to enable us to understand the universe, but merely to allow us and our species to survive amid a terrestrial environment in which objects roughly comparable with our own size, weight, and duration are of chief importance—objects which range in magnitude from a flea or a grain of sand to an elephant, an oak, or a fair-sized hill. We have sense-organs for light, heat, sound, actual contact, and a small number of chemical properties, but, strange to say, none for electricity or magnetism. Our language and our syntax have been developed to enable us to cope with day-to-day life in a semi-civilized world, and little else. When we try to explain things that are more abstruse, we have to talk in terms of analogies and metaphors—or, as the scientist prefers to say, in terms of 'thought-models'; and at times these are all too liable to be misinterpreted.

It is essential to bear these limitations in mind when we are confronted with the efforts made by mystics and sensitives, mediums and parapsychologists, to describe their various observations and the interpretations they put upon them. Their records and their explanations have to be made in terms either of everyday concepts, or of slightly more technical concepts which can be defined at one or two removes by means of such everyday concepts, and which are as a rule little better than the latest fashion in analogies, metaphors, or myths.

Even for our everyday conscious experiences we still have no adequate nomenclature; and beneath it all there is a complicated mechanism of what are variously termed unconscious, subconscious, or subliminal activities of which, from their very nature, we are ordinarily unaware. Nowadays the notion of 'the unconscious' is popularly associated with the name of Freud. But it is to the Cambridge scholar, F. W. H. Myers—the leader of the small group who founded the Society for Psychical Research—that the concept in its broader sense is mainly due. Under this linguistic umbrella he brought together a whole range of puzzling manifestations—the phenomena of trance and mediumship, certain forms of telepathy, the ecstatic visions of the mystic, the inspirations of genius, the plain man's simple 'brain-waves', the complex instincts of lowlier animals, as well as those borderline processes which have attracted the attention of psychiatric and psychoanalytic writers—hypnotism, suggestion, automatism, somnambulism, and ordinary dreams. Unfortunately, the language used by both Myers and Freud has tended to magnify rather than diminish the cryptic and mystifying aspects of the activities involved.

There is yet another set of widespread misconceptions of which the reader should clear his mind before he starts on the later chapters of this book. Most people seem to think that clairvoyance, if it occurs at all, implies what the word taken literally would seem to suggest—'clear seeing', as if the clairvoyant were looking into a lighted room across the road with a pair of magic field-glasses; that the telepathist or 'thought-reader' is able to read the thoughts of others as readily as he reads a book; that 'spirit-messages' are as distinct and explicit as if they were conveyed over the telephone. Here, once again, we are all too prone to forget what a long and delicate chain of processes is involved in ordinary perception, and still more in our ordinary thought processes. In what is called 'extra-sensory perception' the links must be still more tenuous and intricate; and the results more like the blurred murmurings and flickering fragments some of us may remember in the days when wireless, telephony, and television were in the experimental stage.

Whatever may be the explanatory hypothesis which we ourselves provisionally accept, it seems evident that, if we are to gain a progressive understanding of the mental processes involved in these anomalous experiences, our most hopeful line of approach will be to start from what we already know about the ordinary modes of perception and thought, and the more familiar experiences of reverie and nocturnal dreams. Often, I believe, it will prove instructive to apply much the same methods of analysis that Freud adopted in unravelling the 'latent significance', not only of his patients' dreams, petty obsessions, and other pathological symptoms, but also the unconsciously determined thoughts and actions of everyday life. So long as the conduct and the utterances of the hysteric, the paranoiac, and the raving drug-addict were regarded as the signs of divine inspiration or demoniac possession, scientific interpretation and therapeutic treatment were out of the question. As soon as the mists of superstition and the supernatural glamour had been effectively dispelled, it was seen that the erratic mental processes, even of the maddest lunatic, were basically the same as those of ordinary mortals. So, too, with the puzzling phenomena studied in psychical research. And as a beginning, I suggest that, save perhaps for convenience of reference, we might drop the practice of ticketing such occurrences as 'extra-', 'super-', 'trans-', 'sub-', or 'ab-'. They are certainly 'psychical', in the sense that the everyday activities of perception, feeling, and thought are psychical; but as yet there is no convincing evidence that they are, in the strict meaning of the term, 'para-psychological'.

'Before we can decide what, if anything, we really know,' so a great Indian philosopher has recently said, 'we must discover how we know or seem to know.' And towards this end Mrs Heywood's own analyses furnish a most helpful contribution—one, let us hope, which will quickly be followed by similar studies from equally impartial and self-critical observers. Above all, we must never forget what an 'infinite hive' of unsuspected activities the mind of man has proved to be. In years to come, after we have gleaned a better understanding of the elusive processes at work, we may perhaps go forward to investigate deeper philosophical issues that continually raise their heads, and ask that well worn question—'What, if anything, does all this tell us about reality?'

CYRIL BURT

PART I

General Background

CHAPTER I

The Mental Climate

The question which has always most nagged at humanity is, 'Who are we?', and we grope towards an answer through the experience of every individual.

The aim of this book is to record certain experiences of my own which may have been due to the alleged capacity nowadays known as extra-sensory perception, or E S P for short. Only may: there is no cast-iron evidence that they were. It is safer to call them E S P-*type* experiences, and I do not know of any sure way to explain or interpret them. Nor am I trying to use them to prove or disprove E S P. Things are what they are, I am no missionary, and as Faraday said, the truth will always make itself known in the end.

I shall use the term E S P to stand in a general way for an apparent form of communication between an individual and his surroundings which does not make use of one of the known senses as its medium. It is not an ideal term, for the word perception may be a misnomer since the response to such communication does not always appear to be a conscious one; but the shortened form, E S P, is by now so well known that to avoid it would probably create confusion.

There are several variants of what may be E S P. The best known are telepathy (by which one person seems to respond to the mental state of another), precognition of the future, and impressions of events which are distant in space or belong to the past in time. Whatever its cause, E S P has been reported down the ages and throughout the world, often by practical and well-balanced persons, but as it cannot be exercised to order and as yet no rational explanation for it has been found, it cannot be given a place among respectable media of information like sight or hearing. On the contrary, though often over popular with the simple, to most of the highly educated it is about as welcome as a lady of the streets in a Victorian drawing-room. In fact the general love-hate attitude to it is nearly as curious as the phenomenon itself.

The mental climate created by that attitude has a marked effect on people who have E S P-type experiences, driving some to an almost aggressive credulity and others to an embarrassed scepticism which may well inhibit their power of perception. It certainly raises some uncomfortable problems for anyone who attempts to record personal E S P-type experiences in a detached and impersonal fashion. It is also the background against which all such experiences should be considered. For that reason I will try to convey some idea of it before recording my own.

In 1960 I was asked, somewhat to my surprise, to give a talk on E S P to a group of high-powered, down-to-earth business men, including biochemists, statisticians and other members of the world where science and business meet. Mellowed by an excellent dinner, the audience was kind; it laughed at my little jokes and it did not laugh at my little anecdotes about alleged spontaneous cases of E S P. It even listened politely to the serious experimental evidence for the capacity which, incidentally, is more than prosaic.[1] At the end of the evening several of the group recounted instances of apparent E S P, mainly telepathic, in their own lives, and so interested were they in the subject that the secretary told me that never before had their monthly meeting broken up so late. But I had learnt to allow time for the swing of the pendulum, so I waited a week and then asked the secretary if he thought his friends would give me their experiences in writing, as I was anxious to collect such reports from educated and balanced persons. His

[1] Most of the experimental evidence for E S P consists in guessing the order of thousands of unseen packs of cards in fraudproof circumstances, and getting it right, not exactly, but to an extent which according to statisticians, is of an order of probability comparable to that of a monkey tapping out a poem by chance on a typewriter. Some of these experiments have been described by the investigators who made them, notably by Dr J. B. Rhine in *New Frontiers of the Mind* (Faber, 1938) and subsequent books, and by Dr S. G. Soal (with F. Bateman) in *Modern Experiments in Telepathy* (Faber, 1954).

Professor C. D. Broad has recently made an important assessment of all the evidence, both experimental and spontaneous, in *Lectures on Psychical Research* (International Library of Philosophy and Scientific Method, Routledge Kegan Paul, 1962).

answer was the one I expected: 'I am sorry but in the cold light of day they are not prepared to enlarge upon their experiences. I regret having to disappoint you, but I believe such reluctance is quite usual.'

It is, indeed. But why? One partial explanation is that reason itself is now our god—fortunately enough, seeing the morass of superstition from which man has struggled to make it so. But it can be a jealous god, and some of its devotees prefer not to face the fact that much of their own motivation is, from the point of view of surface consciousness, irrational, still less that they may themselves react to influences they can neither detect nor control. On the bright highway of reason they feel secure. Why jump off it into a murky swamp? Moreover, the educated are trained to ignore the irrelevant, and an impression which appears from nowhere and has no connection with one's exterior surroundings or current train of thought seems obviously irrelevant.

Then, too, in the past ESP was associated with the super-natural and magic, and even among the most rational moderns there may well still exist, though deeply buried, an atavistic fear of such uncontrollable forces. 'Us don't believe in ghosts,' said the old countryman, 'but us be mighty feared of 'em.'

Sir Frederick Bartlett records an experiment in which he gave twenty-seven undergraduates a folk tale to read which contained two supernatural elements.[2] Afterwards, at varying intervals, they each had to write down what they remembered of it, and there was a very marked tendency to forget the supernatural elements or rationalize them away. 'There is a superstition in avoiding superstition,' said Francis Bacon, 'when men think to do best if they go furthest from the superstition formerly received.'

A third very natural reason for hostility to ESP is that, as a result of belief in the supernatural and in magic, it has for thousands of years been simulated for the sake of money or power. Its whole history is revoltingly mixed up with fraud. And not only its history. A glance today at popular periodicals dealing with the 'occult' suggests that it still appeals to a persistent superstition. Moreover, to the popular press in general any tall story involving alleged ESP is always 'news', and the 'Vicar Exorcises Headless

[2] Sir Frederick Bartlett, F.R.S., *Remembering* (C.U.P. 1950), p. 65 et seq.

Phantom in Haunted House' type of headline a certain hit. In consequence any well known person who admits to an E S P-type experience runs the risk of sticking his head into a hornets' nest of reporters.[8]

But to the conservative rational mind E S P itself is the worst culprit, for it appears to break the laws of Newtonian science, and only electrons and their relatives can get away with that. Telepathy, for instance, cannot be reconciled with the law that for one object to affect another there must be a transfer of energy between the two, or precognition with the law that an effect can never precede its cause. This unfortunately does not drive the orthodox to wonder whether still youthful humanity already knows all there is to be known about the real nature of time, space and energy. On the contrary, it dismisses E S P *a priori* as irrational and therefore impossible. But it now looks as if to the really great scientist this attitude has begun to appear a little old-fashioned. 'If we are to discern the controlling laws of nature not dictated by the mind,' said Eddington, 'it would seem necessary to escape as far as possible from the cut and dried framework into which the mind is so ready to force everything that it experiences.'[4]

Professor Dingle is another who has his doubts about ignoring experience because it does not obey the rules. 'When,' he says, 'we put experience in its true position as the origin of thought, and not as the effect of emanations from a blind natural machine, we cease to be able to ignore any experience on the ground that it is "unreal" or "illusory". It is just as fit for scientific study as the so-called "real" experiences, and it is the subsequent rationalisation that decides if it is to be differently classified or not.'[5]

It would appear difficult to decide how to rationalize an ex-

[8] The following are extracts from three recent advertisements:
(i) 'Joan the Wad is the Queen of the Cornish Piskies and with whom good luck and good health always attend. History free for 1–/.' Then follows an account of the pools won, the millionaires married and the promotion achieved through 'just that extra luck that faith in Joan brings'.
(ii) 'Mystic's startling Revelation. Direct answers to all your petitions in every emergency.'
(iii) 'Moon Magick will be available again in Britain for Winter Solstice. Magick is our business.'
[4] *The Nature of the Physical World* (C.U.P., 1928), p. 210.
[5] Herbert Dingle, *The Scientific Adventure* (Pitman, 1952), p. 261.

perience if one dared not even look to see what it was like, and, for the most part, that is what seems to happen to the sophisticated if faced with something that might be E S P. They avert their eyes with embarrassment, not to say fear.

Here, for example, are the reactions of two distinguished men to their own experience of visual hallucinations.[6] The first is recorded by Francis Galton in his *Memoirs*. Before doing so he says with gentle irony that in general verbal replies to his inquiry as to the incidence of hallucinations among sane persons 'very often took a form like this. "No, no, I've never had any hallucination." Then, after a pause, "Well, there certainly was one curious thing . . ."' Then he tells us that before a meeting of the Royal Society, Sir Risden Bennett, a Past President of the Royal College of Medicine, *drew him aside* (my italics) and told him that more than once he had seen a man in mediaeval costume come into his study. The man was said by Sir Risden to be 'perfectly distinct in every particular, buttons and all', but 'after a brief time he faded and disappeared. Sir Risden said he felt in perfect health; his pulse and breathing were normal and so forth, but he was naturally alarmed at the prospect of some impending brain disorder. Nothing of the sort had followed'.

Just because no brain disorder followed, did Sir Risden report this interesting experience to his colleagues? No. 'I begged him,' writes Galton, 'to publish the curious case fully . . . but he hesitated; however he did ultimately publish it . . . in some medical paper, signed only with his initials.'

This was in the 1880s, but the mental climate has changed very little. In the 1950s the sister of a well-known scientist confessed to me that she had recently seen an apparition near enough to touch. And, what was worse—she almost whispered this—her distinguished brother had seen it too, no less than three times; and each time at a certain spot it had just faded away! Naturally he did not speak of the figure until she did, and then they found that

---

[6] Nervous recoil from hallucinations has been increased by the debasement of the word to stand only for the *morbid* hallucinations of drink, drugs or disease, but its dictionary definition carries no such implication. It is simply 'any supposed sensory perception which has no objective counterpart'. Ordinary dreams, for instance, are hallucinations, and recent research suggests that we may not do very well without them.

independently they had observed a number of very unusual features about it. Would it be possible to have separate written reports of their experiences? I asked, but the answer once more was, No. I replied that I quite understood, and in any case the figure could well have been an illusion caused by the play of light and shade. Fortunately for me it was less unthinkable for a scientist to experience a hallucination than to be misled by a shadow, and so, after swearing the strictest secrecy as to identity, I got my reports.

Since making the notes for this chapter I was asked to a dinner at which the host and most of the guests were highly qualified scientists in their thirties. I was the only amateur present and they very kindly asked me what were my interests. Good food and drink having bolstered up my courage, I reminded myself that I had no scientific reputation to lose and admitted to E S P. Fortunately the good food and drink had done its work on the experts too, and one of them suddenly confessed that, when at a very difficult crossing of the ways, a visionary figure had appeared with instructions what to do. 'Did you do what it told you?' I asked, fascinated.

'Oh, yes, at once. I knew the figure was right.'

'Why didn't you tell me this before?' asked our host, who was the speaker's close friend.

'I couldn't. You were a scientist.'

'But I'm very interested in these experiences,' exclaimed the host.

'Then why didn't you tell me so?'

'How could I? You were a scientist.'

It must be remembered, however, that not E S P alone but any phenomenon which does not fit in with current beliefs is always liable to be unpopular. Copernicus assumed that he would be 'hissed out of court' for his idea that the earth revolved round the sun and Charles Darwin said that to confess to disbelief in the immutability of species was like confessing to a murder. 'The mind,' says Wilfred Trotter, 'likes a new idea as little as the body likes a strange protein and resists it with similar energy. It would not perhaps be too strong to say that a new idea is the most quickly acting antigen known to science. If we watch ourselves honestly we shall often find that we have begun to argue against a new idea, even before it was completely stated.'[7]

Many discoverers of unexpected properties of the physical world have been laughed at, much as students of E S P are laughed at today. Leibnitz himself wrote of the theory of gravity: 'That one body should attract another with no intermediary is not so much a miracle as a sheer contradiction, for 'tis to suppose a body can act in a place where it is not.' And when it came to research into electro-magnetic phenomena, Galvani was ridiculed at first for his interest in the twitching legs of a frog, Röntgen for his discovery of X-rays and Becquerel for suggesting that uranium salts could emit radiation. Then, in 1901, came Marconi's wild idea of sending wireless signals from Cornwall to Newfoundland. Men still living remember how contemporary scientists laughed at that. 'The earth is round,' they said, 'and radio waves go straight.' One of them remarked that Marconi's idea was as silly as that of telepathy. Soon afterwards the Heaviside layer was discovered.

Nowadays electro-magnetic phenomena form part of the basic material of science, but the study of E S P has been left very near the post. I have mentioned several reasons for this: dislike of vulgar publicity, disgust at superstition and fraud, a hangover from fear of the supernatural and from the belief that Newtonian laws must be all-embracing, and a natural suspicion of any phenomena which do not fit into the accepted pattern. And there are still others. One is that spontaneous E S P seems to occur very seldom, or it may be that it is only noticed very seldom. In a recent article Professor Polanyi has discussed our tendency to overlook things that are unprecedented.[8] 'Having,' he says, 'no clue to them we do not see them. Darwin has described how the Fuegians crowded wonderingly around the rowing boat which took his party ashore from the *Beagle* but failed to notice the ship itself lying at anchor in front of them. Scientists are, of course, as liable to this failing as the Fuegians were. . . . But we must not blame

[7] Quoted from *The Collected Papers of Wilfred Trotter* (O.U.P.) by Professor W. I. B. Beveridge in *The Art of Scientific Investigation* (Heinemann, 1951), p. 105.

[8] Michael Polanyi, 'The Unaccountable Element in Science', *Philosophy*, January, 1962.

them for this for the craving to find strands of permanence in the tumult of changing appearances is the supreme organon for bringing our experience under intellectual control.'

A further and all too human reason for the recoil from E S P of many contemporary scientists comes out in a conversation with the late Hans Reichenbach, a leading mathematical logician and philosopher, which Mr Arthur Koestler records in his autobiography. When Koestler said that he had become interested in Dr Rhine's work on E S P Reichenbach replied that E S P was 'all hokum'. 'I said,' writes Koestler, 'that I did not think so—at least the statistical evaluation of the experiments seemed to show relevant results (meaning that they seemed to confirm the existence of telepathy and kindred phenomena). Reichenbach smiled and asked: "Who has checked the statistics?" I said: "R. A. Fisher in person." (Fisher is one of the leading contemporary experts in probability calculus.)'

Mr Koestler had to repeat this because at first Reichenbach did not appear to take it in. When he did he went pale and exclaimed, 'If that is true it is terrible, terrible. It would mean that I would have to scrap everything and start from the beginning.'[9]

On the whole, then, it is hardly surprising that only a small number of thinkers with reputations to lose are prepared—indeed can afford—to study the evidence for E S P, much less admit its validity. (One brilliant man is said to have lost a Chair by doing so.) Nor is it surprising that most of these do not indulge in speculation about the way it works, but still confine themselves to the question: Does it work at all? Is it a genuine natural phenomenon? This question was first asked in modern times by a group of Cambridge intellectuals, and in 1882, to try to answer it, they founded the Society for Psychical Research, commonly known as the S.P.R. Henry Sidgwick was its first President. He had no illusions about the task he had set himself. 'My highest ambition in psychical research,' he said, 'is to produce evidence which will drive my opponents to doubt my honesty or veracity. I think that there is a very small minority of persons who will *not* doubt them, and that, if I can convince them, I have done all that I can do. As regards the majority even of my own acquaintances, I should claim no more than an admission that they were considerably surprised to find *me* in the trick.'[10]

Among other pioneer members of the S.P.R. were Lord Rayleigh and Professor J. J. Thomson. It is interesting that these two great scientists also supported Röntgen and Becquerel respectively when at first their improbable discoveries about radiation were doubted by other experts.

Owing to the mental climate *vis-à-vis* E S P, the findings of the S.P.R., the American S.P.R. and other pioneer researchers are less well known than they should be and are often misrepresented. It was in the hope of contributing a fraction towards dispassionate consideration of their work that in 1959 I wrote a short nontechnical introduction to it, strictly from the point of view of the question: What evidence is there for E S P? I fell over backwards to make this a down-to-earth record of hard facts, which had been checked and rechecked by competent investigators. Speculation, introspection and imagination were sternly ruled out. At this I felt somewhat smug, but not for long. 'Very nice,' said a well known psychologist who was brave enough to be interested in E S P, 'But it shows only half the picture, E S P as seen by an investigator from the *outside*. I want the point of view of the percipient.[11] Write another book. Give your own experiences.'

Coming from the source it did, this was very flattering. But it also frightened me. What would such a book involve? First, E S P apart, it would have to be introspective. But introspective material cannot be measured or even assessed statistically, and we are all being conditioned nowadays to accept the view that for science such material cannot exist. Especially anything to do with consciousness or minds. In the *British Journal of Statistical Psychology*, for instance, I had just been reading a quotation from advice given by two psychologists to their colleagues: 'Keep well within the bounds of Newtonian science, since it is the surest way to avoid the invalid postulation of subjective qualities or occult

[10] *Presidential Addresses to the S.P.R.* 1882–1911, p. 50.
[11] Since this was said to me Professor E. R. Dodds has suggested experient as a better word than percipient, because, he says—and my own limited experience certainly confirms this—the person who reacts to an extra-sensory signal does not always perceive it. What reaches his consciousness may simply be 'a motor impulse accompanied by an appropriate "feeling tone".' *Journal* S.P.R., September, 1962, p. 354.

entities like consciousness and mind.' Clearly introspection *plus* E S P would not be fashionable.[12]

For myself, having, as I said, no scientific reputation to lose, that did not matter. But I do have scientifically trained friends who concentrate on chasing the *evidence for* E S P in a strictly orthodox manner. Their orthodoxy, though, has not saved them from working in a chilly no-man's land, sniped at from one side by ardent Sceptics and from the other by equally ardent Believers. The Sceptic pronounces with sublime faith that since E S P *cannot* make sense the only possible conclusion is that people who have produced experimental evidence for it, however coercive that seems to be, must either have been led up the garden path by frauds, or be frauds themselves.[18] But the ardent Believer's faith is yet more sublime. To him not only does E S P make sense, but from it he takes a wild leap forward to the conviction that he can communicate with the discarnate on Higher Planes. Not long ago a lonely widower, Mr Black, assured me that a spiritualist medium he knew had contacted a spirit who was looking for a Mrs White. 'Obviously by Mrs White she meant me!' he cried rapturously, and, poor man, he thought me a hard-hearted bone-headed Sceptic to doubt such splendid evidence that he had renewed contact with his beloved wife.

Psychical researchers try not to let this double emotional barrage affect their search for facts, but the Sceptics are backed by big battalions and the researchers would be more than human did they not lean over backwards to avoid being classed, if not with the double-dealers, then with the Mr Blacks. And, of course, they

[12] The layman notes with surprise that it seems to be psychologists rather than physicists who are prone to dismiss the concept of consciousness. Eddington and Schroedinger, for instance, took it as essential, and so does Heisenberg. And E. P. Wigner, Professor of Theoretical Physics at Princeton, remarked recently, 'For reasons that are not quite clear, the phenomenon of consciousness has become tabu in scientific circles. Nevertheless . . . even the laws of quantum mechanics itself cannot be formulated, with all their implications, without recourse to the concept of consciousness.'
From an essay in *The Logic of Personal Knowledge*, a *festschrift* for Professor Michael Polanyi (Routledge Kegan Paul, 1961) p. 232.

[18] Professor H. J. Eysenck has pointed out that if fraudulent experimentation is the answer to the positive evidence for E S P it implies that there is a 'gigantic conspiracy involving some thirty University departments all over the world and several hundred respectable scientists in various fields'. *Sense and Nonsense in Psychology* (Pelican Books, 1957), p. 131.

themselves meet with a discouraging amount of mal-observation, faulty memory, false deduction, unconscious inference and wishful thinking in people who claim to have experienced E S P. It is natural enough then, even when they accept its existence in theory, that they will not touch an alleged spontaneous case of it with a pair of tongs unless that case is buttressed by cast-iron evidence.

Herein lay my difficulty. I had learnt at first hand that nature does not trouble about cast-iron evidence. She produces an E S P-type experience when it suits her, in other words when conditions are favourable, whether or not they are such as to make buttressing possible. Sometimes too the experience is so trivial that it is ignored until found to correspond with a distant event; and from the evidential point of view that is too late. Or, on the contrary, it may be so disturbing as to leave even the critically minded experient in no mood to care whether it was buttressed or not. Yet I felt sure that were I to include inadequately buttressed cases, even if only as *psychological experiences recorded by an experient and not as evidence for E S P proffered by an investigator*, some researchers would be sure to feel that I was letting down the side. I understood that defensive attitude very well, not only on account of emotional extremist exaggerations by both Sceptics and Believers, but because too many books are published, dressed up as works of serious investigation, in which leaky evidence is put forward as *proof* of E S P. That kind of pseudo-science exasperates the genuinely scientific mind and does more harm to serious psychical research than the juiciest outpourings of the most ardent Mr Blacks. I did not want to appear to add to it. Moreover, autobiographies written by pseudo-experients whose imagination at least is outsize are very profitable. If I wrote the book I had been asked for, would I be classed with these inventors of psychic wonders?

Then *amour propre* came up with another deterrent idea. To the outer world such a book might suggest that I belonged to a Cult; and, partly from intellectual snobbery, partly from a genuine fear of any kind of dogma, I fly from Cults as a mouse will fly from cats. But most experients do not. If, as usually happens, the orthodox laugh at their experiences, many of them fly to a Cult for shelter, wisely perhaps from the psychological point of view, for it gives them a sense of security and a mental framework in which those experiences are allowed to make sense. Such shelter-seeking is so widespread that anyone who dares to confess, say, to the experience of talking with apparently discarnate persons, however much he prefaces his confession by insisting that he finds the idea of survival after death to be almost unthinkable, will surely be branded a Mr Black. And heaven help him if he admits to having bodily reactions to apparent invisible stimuli; he is labelled at once a disciple of Madame Blavatsky, and credited with being able to take the idea of auras, chakras and astral bodies in his stride. Some people think, too, that even to mention E S P is practically to traffic with the devil. A gay and highly competent relative of mine said to me the other day in a sepulchral voice, 'Are you still writing books about the supernatural!'

What it all comes to is that an experient is seldom allowed to be a humble neutral inquirer, to say quite simply, 'I've had such and such an *experience*. I don't know what caused it or how to interpret it and should be grateful for help.'

I mulled over all these difficulties for nearly three years, feeling more and more in a fog and less and less inclined to embark on a personal record. And yet—thousands of other people had experienced apparent extra-sensory communication with something outside themselves. So many experiences must indicate something, and if they should turn out to be more than subjective, something perhaps of major importance. But that in its way was another deterrent. As if my trivial little experiences could contribute anything towards a major discovery. At last, when I had practically given up all idea of such nonsense, fortune came to my aid in the shape of three illuminating passages which I happened to read one after another at the right moment. One was by Professor Beveridge on research in general. 'Discoveries,' he wrote, 'are made by giving attention to the slightest clue. The aspect of the scientist's mind which demands convincing evidence should be reserved for the proof stage of the investigation. In research an attitude of mind is required for discovery which is different from that required for proof, for discovery and proof are distinct processes.'[14]

[14] W. I. B. Beveridge, *The Art of Scientific Investigation* (Heinemann, 1950), p. 32.

The second was on biology by Sir Julian Huxley. 'It has become clear,' he wrote, 'that animals do not reveal the higher possibilities of their nature and behaviour nor the full range of their individual diversity, except in conditions of freedom. Captivity cages minds as well as bodies and rigid experimental procedure limits the range of performance.'[15]

And the third was by Professor Sir Cyril Burt on the study of ESP itself. 'By placing the emphasis on the paranormal character of the phenomena instead of on their psychological character, students of psychical research have to some extent impeded the scientific study of the problems involved and delayed the acceptance of results already achieved.'[16]

These three remarks blew away my fog. The slightest clue . . . Captivity cages minds as well as bodies . . . Students of ESP have delayed research by playing down the psychological aspects of the phenomena. . . . Why had I been fussing? Whether or not ESP-type experiences were of interest, whether the person reporting them was a bore, an exhibitionist or a fool, was not his affair. Nor was he even concerned with the question: Does ESP occur? His role was to be an articulate duck-billed platypus or greylag goose and to report his experiences honestly, however absurd they might seem. When Galton asked a young woman her reaction to the word 'Boat', her reply was trivial enough: 'I see a boat and in it there are some women dressed in blue.' But that reply was one of Galton's clues to visual imagery. With luck my material might provide similar clues, at least to the experimental conditions in which ESP might best be sought. And if it did not, it might still be instructive in the same fashion as the dreams of normal people or the delusions of the insane.

Insensibly, during those three years, a further incentive to write a personal record had been growing. As a result of my first book I had met a number of people who had bottled up experiences similar to mine because, they said, their friends looked on that kind of thing as something nasty in the woodshed, and would probably think them mad. And some of them feared, poor things, that the friends might perhaps be right. Others misinterpreted

[15] Sir Julian Huxley, Introduction to *King Solomon's Ring* by Konrad Lorenz.
[16] 'Physicality and Psi', *Journal of Parapsychology* XXV, 1961 (i), p. 31.

E S P-type experiences, which to me seemed quite natural and harmless, in so lurid a fashion that they too feared for their sanity. I asked an enlightened psychiatrist his views on one such apparent misinterpretation, and he replied that had it been told to a strictly orthodox medical adviser it could well have landed the experient in a mental hospital, 'from which,' he added gravely, 'he might never have come out.'

Obviously bottling-up does not always produce such dire effects, but it is never a life-giving process and it is, perhaps, yet another sign that there is something in the present mental climate which forces many people to function with only part of themselves. The rest of their psyche, which in the old days would also have been nourished by religion, now seems to be locked away in a cellar and starved. And the starving will grab at any food available. Hence the spread of cults and popular occultism. For some temperaments they do provide food of a kind, and they can be, *faute de mieux*, a safety valve—a safety valve that appears to be needed seeing that one Spiritualist centre alone in London reported that during the year 1961 it had 82,000 visitors.

But if E S P is a normal capacity like sight or hearing, it needs to be treated as normal, to be brought up into the open air, to be freed, not only from strange and sometimes unhealthy interpretations and beliefs, but also from the withering disapproval of people who have not experienced it.

At last, then, I had reached the starting point. Now the problem facing me was: What to write? It seemed clear that to describe each experience in isolation only made sense if the question asked was the traditional one: Was this a case of E S P? If that were changed to psychological questions, such as: How did the experience appear to the experient? What seemed to occasion it? Did it throw any light on an inter-personal relation?, then its setting would be needed as well. Moreover, judging from the autobiographies of certain 'star' experients, that setting must not be too narrow, for even the loves, fears, shocks and frustrations of childhood seemed to have influenced their later exercise of apparent E S P. It looked, in fact, as if I should have to write about a good deal of my own life. This was a shock; it went dead against my upbringing. As a girl I had once asked my devoted mother, who was intensely shy, if she would please ask some nice people

I had just met to the house as I did so want to see them again. She looked staggered. 'What reason have you to suppose,' she said, 'that they could want to see you?'

However, I reminded myself that no greylag goose would suffer from egocentric inhibitions, and carried on.

CHAPTER II

Byeways to Consciousness

If the ESP-type experiences of any individual are to be more than a string of pointless anecdotes they must be seen against three backgrounds: the mental climate in relation to ESP itself, which I have already tried to sketch; certain characteristics of apparent spontaneous ESP in general, and the relevant aspects of the individual's own life. The next three chapters will be concerned with the second background, spontaneous ESP in general.

When writing about this debatable subject from the evidential point of view, investigators safeguard themselves—very rightly—by the constant repetition of such words as purported, ostensible, alleged or apparent, but to do so in this kind of record would get on the nerves of both writer and reader. From now on, then, I shall leave the reader to insert a safeguarding word whenever he feels inclined, and I shall write as if—only *as if*—ESP were a natural though seldom observed faculty in human beings. At the same time I do not want to claim that all the correspondences between my impressions and events about which I did not know by sensory means at the time, or even all those which are recorded in this book, were necessarily examples of ESP. Some could have been due to a kind of inferential process, perhaps subconscious: some obviously could have occurred by chance. Readers will decide for themselves whether all are likely to have done so. This is presumably possible. One must remember too that, as Bacon said, men mark when they hit, and never mark when they miss. As an investigator I should try to remain neutral. As experient I am inclined to give them the benefit of the doubt, both because of their unexpectedness and of my own feelings at the time, and because they conform to psychological patterns which I have come to recognize.

Another difficulty, when writing such a record as this, is that one has to use words which for specialists have narrower meanings than the generally accepted ones, or which even stand for something considered by many experts to be non-existent. The most

tricky of these words are will, mind, consciousness and the subconscious. I shall use the first three as the man in the street uses
them, but with no assumptions as to exactly what they stand for,
and subconscious simply as meaning an area of the psyche beyond
the threshold of consciousness, but with no implication of 'above'
or 'below', of gold-mine or rubbish heap.

The essential point to note about spontaneous E S P-type impressions which correspond with mundane events is that this correspondence need not be literal. The process seems to be that
an extra-sensory signal—for want of a better word—is received
at a subconscious level of the personality, and that sometimes,
though not always, an overt reaction to it then occurs or an impression emerges to surface consciousness. Here may be a clue
to the infrequency of observed E S P, for this emergence does
not appear to be an easy or straightforward affair. The main
difficulty seems to be a kind of barrier, a censorship, which E S P
has to evade. So too, on occasion, does material which has been
acquired by sensory means and then forgotten or repressed for
emotional reasons. It may be, at least partly, to achieve this evasion that E S P-type material sometimes emerges obliquely, by
means of an associated idea or a symbol, or merely as an impulse
to action. To make detection yet harder, it can also get mixed up
with irrelevant material from the experient's own subconscious.
As a result of all this even he can fail to recognize or can misin-
terpret what is being conveyed, much as a dreamer can miss the
latent content of a dream, and it is obvious that for investigators
seeking *evidence for* E S P, who require exact correspondence between an extra-sensory impression and the event to which it
purports to refer, such material is anything but satisfactory. But
nature cares nothing for what investigators think satisfactory, and
E S P seems to be a far more subtle and complex affair than the
plain hit or miss that they would like it to be. Professor H. H.
Price has commented that the telepathic variant of E S P is 'more
like an infection than like knowledge',[1] and Gilbert Murray, who
came nearer to exercising elaborate telepathy to order than anyone else whose attempts have been systematically recorded, once
said of it, 'As far as my own experience goes it does not feel quite

[1] *Philosophy* 15 (1940), p. 372.

like cognition or detection: it is more like the original sense of the word sympathy (συμπάθεια), the sharing of a feeling or "co-sensitivity". I seem to be passive and feel in a faint shadowy way the feeling or state of mind of someone else.' This is very close to Keats' remark about imagination, that it works by a sympathetic identification with the object contemplated. Who then is to locate the borderline between sensory and extra-sensory perception? Who is to say where imagination stops and telepathy begins?

Telepathy seems to be the most widely experienced of ESP-type phenomena, and Professor C. D. Broad has made an illuminating analysis of it which for me throws a flood of light on most of the experiences I have had myself or seen in others.[2] Indeed, many of them would have gone unnoticed or made little sense without it. He points out that for one person to be telepathically affected by another does not mean that both are receiving the *same* sensory impact from the outer world or both visualizing the *same* image. For this reason he prefers the term telepathic interaction to telepathy, since it conveys better that although A's thought or experience may be the cause of B's, their experiences need not resemble each other at all closely.

A whole string of implications, he says, follow from this. First of all, telepathic interaction may often be taking place, or it may even be continuous, without being noticed, for B need not realize that an event in his own mind has been telepathically induced by A. He may only feel a change of mood or even a mere sensation. (I will give examples of this later.)

Another point made by Professor Broad is that for B to notice the impact from A, it must be discontinuous enough from his own immediate past to surprise him. We are often aware, he says, of an image or thought in our minds which has no conscious ancestor, but oddly enough it seldom surprises us enough to ask how or why it got there. To put this in concrete terms: if I had a telepathic impression that my husband was drinking coffee for breakfast, then, however genuine it was, I would have no means of recognizing it as such, since I expect him to drink coffee for breakfast. If, on the contrary, I had an impression that he was drinking vodka, I should be extremely surprised, and if this was

[2] *Religion, Philosophy and Psychical Research* (Routledge Kegan Paul, 1953).

afterwards found to be correct I should feel that it might have been telepathic.

Another factor making against surprise, as Professor Broad also points out, is that B's experience can never be occasioned by A's alone, but always in part by his own past and present as well. Finally, to recognize the interaction as such, A and B would have to know each other, and one of them would have to feel that his experience was interesting enough to mention it. What all this comes to is that even if telepathic interaction is continuous, it is only likely to be noticed in special circumstances which seldom arise.

To an experient, light on the emergence of subconscious material is also thrown from an unexpected and unorthodox source, Feda, the Control of a famous spiritualist medium of unquestioned integrity, Mrs Osborn Leonard. 'Control' is the name given by spiritualists to the personality which replaces a medium's normal consciousness when he or she falls into a trance. Whether it is, as spiritualists believe, a discarnate entity, or, as most of us think, a split-off bit of the medium's own personality, does not matter in this context. In either case Feda herself can be called an 'Emerger', and her views on the problem tally with the E S P-type experiences of non-spiritualists; so they can usefully be considered entirely irrespective of spiritualist beliefs.

Feda gets communications which she believes come from discarnate persons. But the point of interest here is not their source, but the manner in which she receives them. She says they take many forms. She may seem to herself to hear words or other sounds, she may see written words or imitative or symbolic pictures, or she may have feelings of, say, coldness or roughness. She says that she finds it much easier to receive impressions in the form of symbolic visual images than in the form of words. But she adds—Feda is as transparently honest as Mrs Leonard—that she often makes mistakes when interpreting these symbols.

On their side Feda's purported communicators have definite views as to how they convey information to her, and these, like Feda's own comments, throw light on the E S P-type experiences of non-spiritualists. Suppose, says Professor Broad in a summary of these views, that it is a question of conveying a message about a horse. They explain that they might say the word horse; or produce telepathically an auditory or visual image of the word in Feda's mind; or an image of the horse itself; or a symbolic image of, say, a jockey with a whip. Or, finally, they might telepathically convey the idea of a horse, without the use of words or images of any kind. This is of particular interest to me as most of my impressions seem to be of that imageless nature. The 'communicators' say that it is harder to produce actual sensations of exterior sound in Feda than to convey to her telepathically the image of a word or object, or an imageless idea. One of them also draws an interesting distinction between himself projecting an idea or image into her mind and her playing the active role and reading his mind. If she does this, he says, she may take up some quite unimportant thought, which has nothing to do with what he is trying to communicate, and develop this on her own account.[3]

People who have taken a hallucinogenic drug may have noted a similar process in themselves. When under mescalin, for instance, I was able to observe that a word said by someone present sent me scurrying along a train of associations—actually living them—and this, unless I opened my eyes, I had no power to cut short. The word tea, for instance, landed me in a tea garden in the East, where laughing girls were picking the leaves from bushes, and I ended that train of associations, *via* a China clipper and sailors with pigtails, among mermaids swimming through waving seaweed deep at the bottom of the sea.

But the devious routes which subconscious material may take to consciousness cannot be made clear by description only. They must be illustrated. For that reason I will give a few examples of the emergence of material which had been consciously acquired and then repressed or forgotten, and also of material which appears to have reached the subconscious directly by extra-sensory means.

Not all extra-sensory signals are forced to emerge by devious routes, however, and for comparison I will first give two which appeared undisguised and with only one slight distortion. The difference between these two is that in the first case a telepathic message was consciously 'sent' and in the second the experient

[3] This analysis is summarized from an article on 'The Phenomenology of Mrs. Leonard's Mediumship,' by Professor C. D. Broad, in the *Journal of the American Society for Psychical Research*, April, 1955.

picked up in advance a request which the 'sender' intended to make to her later by sensory means. Incidentally the two impressions also illustrate the type of case in which seekers for evidence of ESP dare to take a mild interest, for the first was mentioned to an observer and they were both acted upon before the information they gave could have reached the experient normally. Moreover, the first contains more than one item, and so is the less likely to have been a chance coincidence—though the coincidences which can occur by chance are quite remarkable.[4]

The incident took place in November 1944. My husband sent me a message from Belgium that I was to expect him to arrive on leave at Victoria Station the following Wednesday at 8 p.m. As we lived quite near I decided to await him at home with as good a dinner as rationing would permit, for in those days trains were very erratic and I saw no point in hanging about for ages in the cold. I was working rather hard at the time and on the Wednesday felt tired out, so, in the hope of being a less dreary object when he arrived, I lay down at half-past six for a short rest. About ten minutes later what I can only describe as a wave of inner pressure flooded over me, to telephone the station and check the time of the train. At first I did not connect this with my husband, and as it seemed idiotic I tried to ignore it. But it would not be ignored. Exasperated, I rolled off the bed and telephoned, to learn that the train was due, not at eight, but shortly after seven. Then I got a further impression: my husband was wanting me to go to the station, try to get a porter, and be ready to carry small things for him myself. At this I flung on my clothes and ran downstairs, for there was little time; but before going out I told some friends who were staying with me, Mr and Mrs G. N. M. Tyrrell, that I thought my husband had sent these messages, and would they please note that I had told them so before I saw him. Mr Tyrrell was at that time President of the S.P.R., and I felt rather smugly that this time I had got the perfect witness to what I felt sure was a case of ESP. Outside a stranger was turning away from his car to enter the house opposite, and I tore across

---

[4] Last week, for instance, I had to choose between telephoning to my local post office or overseas telegrams for some information. I chose the post office, Sloane, 1830. The call misrouted and I got overseas telegrams, 557.

the road and said to him, 'Please take me to Victoria or I shall miss my husband who is coming home on leave!'

He looked as astonished as I felt at such odd behaviour; but he was very kind and took me, and by good luck I was able to catch a porter and reach the platform just as the train, unexpectedly punctual, steamed in. 'Don't speak,' I cried as my husband stepped out of it, and though he looked somewhat taken aback at this welcome home from the wars he remained obediently silent. I went on to ask him whether he had in fact sent me the messages which I thought I had received, and then he understood. 'Yes,' he said. 'On arrival at Folkestone I realized that I had given you continental, not British, time and that porters would be very hard to get. I had been asked to bring some extra small packages home from G.H.Q., and had more than I could carry alone. As the post office was shut and the telephone booths had a mile-long queue, all I could do was to send you a mental message while I was coming up in the train.' Again I felt smug. My only mistake had been to translate his feeling that there might not be a porter into orders to get him one.

Some points are worth noting here. I will try to bring out their possible significance later. (1) I did not get my husband's message until I lay down and relaxed, although from his account he had begun 'sending' it earlier. (2) At first I did not realize that it came from him. I merely felt a compulsive urge to telephone. (3) The situation was a valid, not an artificial one; that is, he only 'sent' the message mentally because no other means of communication were available. (4) It was also emotional, for this was his first leave since the Normandy landings, and since, from my point of view, the sense of his being in constant danger had decreased.

We both wrote independent accounts of the incident, and the Tyrrells confirmed mine. But even so, the seeker after cast-iron evidence would have to say that I only took the action which my husband might have been expected to want. From the experient's point of view, however, no outside investigator could obtain all the evidence; he could not feel the apparently senseless inner pressure to get up and telephone, when all I wanted to do was to lie flat on my bed and doze. And an ardent Sceptic, of course, always has a way out. My husband, the Tyrrells and I might have gone into a huddle to concoct a lie.

My next example of straightforward E S P dates back to the spring of 1926. My husband came in early from the War Office and said during tea, on the spur of the moment, 'I've just heard that I can't have my leave till the autumn. What about taking a house in Wimbledon for the summer to get some tennis in the evenings? We might ask Mary (a friend who lived there) to have particulars sent us from the local agent.'

But Mary, whom we had known do this sort of thing before, did not wait to be asked. By the first post next morning came a sheaf of houses 'to let' from the Wimbledon Hamptons, and we also got a message from her that, having picked up my husband's wish as she walked home from work, she had turned into the local Hamptons which was on her way and had them sent to us.

Now for oblique, as opposed to undisguised, emergence of sub-conscious material. Whether the source of that material is sensory or extra-sensory, the methods it uses to reach consciousness are much the same. Here, for instance, is a case in which a name which had simply been forgotten was brought back by means of an associated idea.

In 1960 I asked the editor of the S.P.R. *Journal*, Mr G. W. Fisk, if he could remember the name of a man who about ten years before had sent in a case which I wanted to check.

'No,' he said, and then added laughing. 'But give my subconscious half an hour and I'll tell you.' Within twenty minutes he rang up. 'I've got it,' he said. 'After I left the telephone the words, "Fairy Queen, Fairy Queen", kept repeating themselves in my head, and as I had been thinking about no such personage I felt it might be a tip and looked for associations. The obvious one being Spenser I looked that up in the *Journal* index. The name you want is Spence.'

Forgotten knowledge can also emerge obliquely by means of an automatism. During the Second World War Theodora Bosanquet, at that time Literary Editor of *Time and Tide*, and I agreed that we would try to get some first hand knowledge of automatisms by working a ouija board together once a week.[5]

---

[5] A ouija board is a flat polished sheet of wood, about eighteen inches by twelve, which has the alphabet written in a wide half circle along one edge. On this board a pointer, in the shape of a smaller heart-shaped bit of wood mounted on three castors, can slip about, and if two or more persons lay

We assumed that what the pointer wrote originated in her sub-conscious or mine, but we also felt it conceivable that the two might collaborate telepathically. We did not take seriously the spiritualist explanation that the board's remarks came from an outside entity, although to carry on a conversation with a bit of wood with any zest one has to suspend criticism and dramatize to oneself that they do.

Theodora came in on the morning of VE Day, 1945, and, as usual, we asked the board what it wanted to talk about. The reply was prompt: 'The sixth noun in *Hamlet*.' Neither of us had the faintest recollection of what that was and we were thoroughly surprised when it turned out to be 'relief', in the sentence, 'For this relief much thanks'. Apt enough for VE Day. But what are the implications? Did one or both of us subconsciously remember *Hamlet* by heart? If so, why count up the nouns and bring the word to the surface in that circuitous way? Was it just to get past the censor, or were our subconscious selves, which usually treated our surface selves tolerantly as half-witted infants, having yet one more joke at their expense? Incidentally this case shows how easily re-emergent long-forgotten knowledge could be mistaken in all honesty for E S P. It suggests that an item seen, but not consciously observed, on, say, the back page of somebody else's evening paper in a train, might be brought up *via* an automatism many years later. The person who did this could then be credited with remarkable E S P, and even he would have no idea that he was cheating.

Next, for comparison, is a trivial instance of what could have been E S P emerging in a similar fashion to the words Spenser and relief. A writer, whose line was witty modern comedy, said to me one day, 'You'll never guess about whom I'm thinking of writing a play.' I replied instantly, 'Oliver Cromwell,' much to my surprise, for that earnest character was the last, I should have thought, to interest him. 'No,' he said, 'but it's about Prince Rupert in his struggle with Cromwell.'

Considered alone by an investigator, this trivial half-hit cries

their fingers lightly on it, it will sometimes point from letter to letter making words and even sentences. These may give information which is not known to the conscious minds of the experimenters and which very occasionally seems never to have been known to them at all.

aloud to be labelled fortuitous, but again an experient has to take his own experience into account. I had made other direct hits on this friend's plans or situations (I will give some later); and, what to me counts for something, on looking back I have discovered a thread of plausible motivation for them. Paradoxically, an investigator would take a direct hit on Prince Rupert more seriously than the associated idea of Cromwell; but I should not, for Prince Rupert was a romantic personality who, to my mind, could well have appealed to this writer, whereas Cromwell was austere, and to suggest him did not make sense.

In the last chapter I mentioned that subconscious material sometimes emerges by means of symbolic visual images. Here are two illustrations. I do not know what to label the first one. Not long ago I read of some laboratory rats which were allowed to choose between identical bowls of food, one of which contained apparently undetectable trace elements necessary to health while the other did not. The rats always chose the first. Here I seem to have behaved rather like the rats, but what kind of faculty we either of us used I cannot guess.

In 1928, after nursing my outsize baby for nearly three months, I began to suffer a most distressing combination of nausea and extreme hunger, which made no sense at all for I was perfectly well. My doctor failed to help, I got worse and worse, and at last, exasperated, I sat down quietly to think the thing out for myself. Then I observed that an image of the chalk track, which used to run on to the downs from the village of Rottingdean, was hanging before my inner eye, and I realized that it had been on the fringe of my consciousness for a day or two, but I had ignored it. Now I asked myself, 'Why do I see that track when the part of Rottingdean I loved ran from the duckpond down to the sea?' At that, inside my mind I heard just one word: 'Calcium.' Calcium! The track was chalk. And my baby's bones were enormous. I got a preparation of calcium from my doctor and the symptoms vanished at once.

It was obvious that this sudden cure might be due to auto-suggestion, but recently a biologist told me that combined hunger and nausea had been recognized by Mellanby in 1938 as symptoms of calcium shortage. That was ten years after my mental image of the chalk track which saved the situation for me.

Here is a parallel case, but this time, from the experient's point of view, of probable E S P, though by others it could well be labelled chance or imagination due to fear. It was told me by Dame Edith Lyttelton. She had become aware of her grandson's death in action by 'seeing' his grand piano—he was a good pianist—covered with a Union Jack. The dual symbolism of the piano is clear enough.[6]

But the image conveying information does not have to be a visual one. Apparently any of the senses can be made use of. My mother occasionally indulged in E S P-type experiences although she did not discuss them. One Sunday I went to visit a friend, an aged Catholic priest, and although I had planned to return early, in the end I stayed on for his evening service. This he liked me to do although I was a pagan. On getting home I said to my mother that I hoped she had not worried at my late return, and she answered peacefully, 'Oh, no, I knew you'd stayed on for the service when a smell of incense flooded the room'.

I have also observed an E S P-type impression take an auditory form. In 1961 to indulge my interest in how such impressions emerge, irrespective of their source, a new friend of mine, a non-professional sensitive, very kindly came and described the way in which impressions floated into his mind as he sat at ease in my drawing-room. He began at once to make comments about a man which tallied excellently with the personality of my brother-in-law, who had been killed in the last war, and about whom I do not think he could have known anything. (In an attempt to check whether his impressions had been picked up telepathically from me, for a moment I made a vivid mental image of another friend who could not have differed more greatly from my husband's brother. The experient at once began to describe such a man.) While speaking of the first man he said, 'I hear the sound of marching feet. I could interpret this as the Changing of the

[6] Shortly after writing this I came on a similar instance of vital information being presented symbolically by apparent E S P in a biography of Francis Bacon by Charles Williams (Arthur Barker, 1933). He says that at the age of eighteen Bacon was in Paris and there one night he dreamt that he saw Gorhambury, the house built by his father, plastered all over with black mortar. He heard shortly afterwards that his father had died suddenly without making the provision for him which he had intended.

Guard, but I *think* it only means that the man I'm talking about was in the army.'

This was correct, and it also illustrated how such correct impressions could be misinterpreted. Had the image of marching feet come to an experient the day after the papers were full of an Aldermaston march, he might well have pictured the man as a pacifist.

The American author, Upton Sinclair, gives some nice examples of misinterpretation in his book on the experimental telepathic transmission of drawings to his wife.[7] She would sometimes draw the right shape and misname it, or get the right title, a pair of legs, for instance, and then draw bird's legs when the target was the forelegs of a deer. It gives the experient a curious feeling of frustration when he feels that he has only got half the information and yet cannot get the rest. I remember my own exasperation when I felt that one experimental target was a 'round thing in the sky'. This was not good enough, for experients had been told to give an exact name to their drawings, and I asked myself, was it the sun or the moon or a planet? No, I felt, it was none of these; but I could not get what it was. It turned out to be a balloon. I mentioned a similar case in my first book on ESP. I felt the target to be a bird. 'Perched or flying?' I asked myself. 'Neither,' I felt. 'Don't be silly, it must be one or the other!' 'Neither.' Annoyed, I drew it flying. The target shortly afterwards was an eagle, hovering, wings half folded, claws retracted, over its nest.

Many experients know that struggle between an ESP-type impression and commonsense. I saw a typical case of it in 1960. A scientist had asked me to have a look at a seaside palmist, because, in spite of his very natural scepticism, he had been interested by the number of correct statements she had made about people he had sent to observe her. At that time my husband and I had been lent a two hundred year old cottage which stood right on the bank of an estuary. At high tide the water lapped against its walls, and we could feed the swans from the windows. What made it yet more enchanting, most of the south wall, downstairs and up, had been replaced by glass. We longed to own it.

[7] Upton Sinclair, *Mental Radio* (Werner Laurie, 1930).

One day, on the spur of the moment, I drove forty miles from the cottage to join the queue at the palmist's booth. When my turn came she made over forty statements, of which many were specific and only two were wrong, and at one point she muttered dreamily (having said that I lived in a town), 'I think you will soon have another home . . . *right on* the water's edge . . . [surprised]. There is *so* much glass . . . such a lot of glass!' Then she pulled herself together and briskly rationalized this into a prophecy that we should one day build ourselves a nice bungalow by the sea.

I mentioned that Mrs Leonard's purported communicators used to complain that her Control, Feda, would fish around in their minds and pick up irrelevant material which then got mixed up with the information they were trying to give. So did the communicators of Mrs Willett, whose E S P was exhaustively studied by the second Lord Balfour.[8] This kind of contamination also occurs in dreams, and analysts attribute it to the stirring up of a complex. It is neatly illustrated by a dream quoted in *The Hidden Springs* by Renée Haynes.[9] In the late thirties a friend of hers went to a literary party in London at which he was so upset by a violent quarrel about the rights and wrongs of the Spanish Civil War that he left early and went home to bed. For a long time he was too restless to sleep and when at last he dropped off he dreamt that his little cat, Mitzi, who lived at his country home, rushed in dressed in Spanish uniform with her ear half torn off. She was screaming miserably, 'Kill me, kill me, I can't stand it!' Being a dream, of course, it was quite natural for poor Mitzi to speak.

Her master woke in a cold sweat and looked at the time. It was about 4 a.m. Later that morning his housekeeper telephoned from the country to say that about 4 a.m. the real Mitzi had come in screaming, with her ear half torn off, and had rushed up to his pillow where she was still lying, still screaming. It is easy enough here to separate the E S P about Mitzi from the emotional origin

[8] Gerald, Earl of Balfour, 'A Study of the Psychological Aspects of Mrs Willett's Mediumship', *Proceedings*, S.P.R., Vol. XVIII, pp. 41/318. The name Mrs Willett was a pseudonym for Mrs Coombe-Tennant, a woman well known in public life.

[9] (Hollis and Carter, 1961).

of the Spanish uniform, but unfortunately such entanglement is not always so obvious nor the E S P so easy to confirm.

I will finish this sketch of modes of emergence of what may be E S P by illustrating two forms of it which, as Professor Broad has pointed out, are particularly hard to detect. One is a simple correspondence of sensations between two persons, in which the experient may not even attribute his own sensation to any cause exterior to himself. A very early case reported to the S.P.R. was of this type. A landscape painter, Arthur Severn, went out sailing one morning while his wife was still asleep. She was awakened later by a blow on her lip so violent that she looked for blood, but to her surprise found none. When her husband returned soon afterwards he was holding his handkerchief to his lip, which was bleeding badly because the tiller had swung over and gashed it when the boat was hit by a sudden gust of wind. (Personal examples of this kind of thing will be given in Chapter IX.)

Finally, telepathic interaction can take the form of an unaccountable change of mood in the experient. I have often experienced this, but have learnt to realize at the time—though not always—that the change might have originated in someone else, usually my husband, and have checked this later. Sometimes I have felt aware of a distant person's mood without sharing it. One Sunday morning this apparent awareness took the oblique form of an almost compulsive urge to telephone the friend of the Cromwell incident and make him laugh. This was so idiotic that I managed, though with difficulty, to resist it: as far as I knew all was well with him, I had nothing to say, and if there is one thing more certain than another about authors, it is that they do not relish being rung up, if they happen to be working, for no reason at all. Still, the compulsion had been so strong that when we met a few days later I asked him casually, 'What were you doing last Sunday morning?'

'Having an attack of black depression,' he replied.

These illustrations of the emergence to consciousness of what may be E S P are far from exhaustive. I have not, for instance, even mentioned the wide subject of apparitions, which are thought by some investigators to be hallucinations induced by the experient in himself to convey a telepathic signal to his conscious mind. But I hope they will be enough to show that E S P is not the simple affair it is often supposed—and indeed required —to be by many who fail to discover it in experimental conditions which sometimes seem to experients specially designed to inhibit it. It is not much good ordering a rainbow to appear when the sun is behind a bank of cloud.

CHAPTER III

Censorship

Most of the illustrations in the last chapter were of telepathic interaction, which I chose because it seems to be the most frequently observed form of E S P. I hope that they will have underlined the question: Why, if telepathy can be as deliberate and straightforward as in the case of my husband's summons to meet him at Victoria, should it ever be otherwise? Is the apparent censorship enough to account for the obliqueness, the images, the symbols?

An additional reason for the images may be that the subconscious, like primitive man, thinks in images rather than by the verbalizations of the highly educated, though Professor H. H. Price has pointed out that in such people image thinking may still be going on all the time, divorced from the stream of surface consciousness. That divorce may be a further reason, over and above intellectual embarrassment, why the highly educated report E S P-type experiences less often than simpler people. They may actually have them less often because the mode of thought to which they have been trained encourages them to ignore 'infections' and 'co-sensitivity' in favour of conscious step-by-step thinking. Also, as I said before, the more rational you are, the more you will tend to reject impressions or impulses to action which have no visibly rational motive. It may be too that any particular experient can only respond to a limited range of signals, as a wine glass can only be set ringing by one particular note. Such limitation may have something to do with interest. The cars which my husband and I pass on the road when we are driving together, for instance, are noted in detail by him, but to me are vague blurs, simply because I prefer to look at the trees or the flowers or the sky.

Whatever may be the real cause, or causes, of the difficulty, one of them does seem to be a kind of censorship. Three famous nonprofessional experients, Mrs Verrall, a Cambridge lecturer, Mrs Holland (pseudonym for Mrs Fleming, Rudyard Kipling's sister) and Mrs Willett all complained of it: that 'something' seemed to inhibit the emergence of knowledge which they felt themselves to possess. Two other 'star' experients, Professor Gilbert Murray and Miss Gertrude Johnson, felt the same.[1]

Dr R. H. Thouless has suggested that on account of ESP's elastic relationship to space and time, to censor it may be biologically useful; a man is more likely to escape death if he can estimate exactly by means of sight and hearing the arrival of a fast car or a hungry tiger.[2] His biological needs also drive him to concentrate his attention primarily on such mundane matters as food, foes and potential mates. 'Thought's the slave of life.' We may be both born and bred to ignore the faint intimations of ESP. From the practical point of view too the development of writing and then of the telegraph, telephone and radio make it less and less needful. Travellers' tales of it have often come from deserts or jungles or arctic wastes where the isolated and unsophisticated inhabitants did not possess those speedy exterior means of communication. In this context it is worth noting that a number of mothers have observed signs of apparent ESP in their young children.[3] These signs decrease as they grow older, and a recent article in the *Journal of Mental Science* suggests that a telepathic link between mothers and very young babies has been observed and may be of biological importance.[4] Very young babies, after all, cannot communicate by means of words.

As an experient I also suspect a further reason for censorship

[1] The work of all these experients is fully reported in the *Proceedings* and *Journal* of the S.P.R. This is also summarized in my book *The Sixth Sense* (Chatto & Windus, 1959), and exhaustively analysed on the philosophical level by Professor C. D. Broad in *Lectures on Psychical Research* (International Library of Science, Routledge Kegan Paul, 1962).

[2] For experimental evidence that both past and future can be apprehended *via* E.S.P. without the experient's being aware that they are not contemporary, see S. G. Soal and R. H. Bateman, *Experiments in Telepathy* (Faber, 1954). Some dreams recorded by J. W. Dunne in *Experiment with Time* (A. and C. Black, 1939) also seem to suggest it.

[3] Peter Scott records an apparent example in his recent autobiography, *The Eye of the Wind.* A few weeks before Captain Scott's ill-fated expedition to the South Pole was discovered, his wife noted in her diary that their two year old son, Peter, had said: 'Amundsen and Daddy both got to the Pole, Mummy, but Daddy has stopped work now.'

[4] Dr Joan Fitzherbert. 'The Role of ESP in Early Childhood', *Journal of Mental Science*, October, 1960.

of E S P. If we were open consciously to all sorts of impressions from all sorts of people all the time, might we not lose that precious sense of personal identity which Westerners so deeply value —men, perhaps, even more than women? Could that be yet one more reason for the evident repulsion it inspires in such men as Dr Hansel and Mr Spencer Brown in England and Dr D. O. Hebb and Dr George Price in America? And why women seem to take more kindly to the idea of it than men? And, according to the general impression, Orientals than Europeans? Even short of losing one's identity, might not a flood of fluid and fleeting impressions be overwhelming partly because one could not organize them into a pattern? A taste of what that would be like can be had by taking a hallucinogen. Under mescalin there were times when I felt just like the Elephant's Child: This is Too Much for me! Why, asks Professor Schroedinger, are our senses so coarse? And he gives an immediate answer. 'If it were not so, if we were organisms so sensitive that a single atom, or even a few atoms, could make a *perceptible* (my italics) impression on our senses— Heavens, what would life be like?'[5]

Moreover, apart from the overwhelming quantity of impressions, might not the quality of some prove too painful to bear? I had a sharp lesson of what this might mean, again under mescalin. With my eyes bandaged I was given a folded letter and asked to comment on the writer, and after holding it for a moment, I threw it away with a shriek. I could not bear it. It made me feel suffocated, stifled, drowned in what at the time I described, sobbing, as the horrible dark brown treacle of a man's anger. And, what was so hateful, I could not cleanse myself of it for a long time. To the doctor who gave me the drug the letter did not convey an impression of such anger and he reported my reaction to its writer. He replied that it fitted the facts. While writing the letter he had been trying to control his violent indignation at a particularly unfortunate incident at his place of work.

Better experients than I have told me that they feel the need for self-defence very acutely. They have had to teach themselves to cut off a kind of E S P which caused them to participate in the thoughts and moods of other people, because they could not en-

[5] Erwin Schroedinger, *What Is Life?* (C.U.P., 1951), p. 7.

dure it. Once, frivolously, I asked a non-professional sensitive what she felt was the reaction of people who were introduced to her, knowing she was gifted with E S P. 'Oh,' she said, 'they all think the same. It's what do *I* think of *them!* So boring!' Then she added, somewhat perversely, 'But you don't give a damn what I think of you!' I felt ashamed of my arrogance, but it was a reminder of how the widespread emergence of E S P would complicate human relations until we had all learnt how to manage our thoughts.

It may be that creative artists are often over-reactive because they are highly endowed with a non-verbal form of E S P which they do not recognize for what it is—which makes it the greater strain. Keats once said that when he was in a room with people 'the identity of everyone in the room begins to press upon me that I am in a very little time annihilated'. And if a sufferer from paranoia also happened to be specially gifted with it, he might pick up the mildly critical thoughts about himself of his friends and neighbours and blow these up into imagined persecution. Or their thoughts might really be more hostile than their outward behaviour. Some years ago I was told—on the anecdotal level—that a patient in a mental hospital was convinced that his mother was trying to murder him. Out of interest, his doctor visited the mother and elicited that, although she had hidden it, she had often wished him dead because he was illegitimate and had damaged her reputation with her neighbours. On having her situation explained to him, so I was told, the patient recovered.

As against the question, What inhibits E S P? there is also its complement, What encourages it? To the experient there seem to be many factors, some in the surrounding conditions, some in himself and, in telepathy, some in the agent. Agent, incidentally, is a term which begs the issue, since it is not known whether he or the experient is the active partner or whether they are both contained in what has been called a common 'psychic field'. I shall use the term simply to denote a person whose state of mind or situation affects another by extra-sensory means. Many experients feel that telepathy is encouraged by such factors as personal affection, including mother-love, by loneliness and frustration, or the need to impress an admired person, or even by common interests. Personally I do better if the situation is a valid, as opposed to a contrived one, and also when it is unexpected, for my conscious attention seems to inhibit the emergence of ESP-type experiences.

I hope that three points have become clear in the last three chapters: that what appear to be extra-sensory impressions are liable to emerge to consciousness by devious byeways; that they better repay study in the light of the physical and psychological settings in which they crop up; and that their frequent triviality does not detract from their instructiveness, since it is the process and not its content that is being considered.

I shall now turn to the third background to my experiences, my own early life.

PART II

Personal Background

CHAPTER IV

Childhood

The next two chapters are an attempt to work out the elements in my childhood and adolescence which may have had some connection with a tendency towards E S P-type experience. Since I could not discover such elements rationally, it seemed best to write down what 'came into my head', hoping that this may have emerged from a level which knows more about them than my conscious self.

One needs something to trigger off a backward flight across the years and this was provided for me last winter by my host at dinner, a famous novelist. 'You must have been hell when you were a child,' he said suddenly, with feeling, between two mouthfuls of duck.

Famous novelists do not make that sort of remark without reason, and I gave it a good deal of thought. That he was right soon became painfully clear, but it also struck me that being hell could perhaps have stimulated the acute sense of solitude and longing for 'real communication' which started young and still endures today. Such longing was absurdly exaggerated and obviously doomed to frustration in outer life. So too was my other basic longing. This was for 'Something Central'—though I did not know what that Something was or where to look for it. And I often ran after very false gods.

The first voice to be heard from the distant Edwardian world of my childhood is our aged Nanny's, 'Naughty girl! What you want is a good licking!' The first picture is of my own legs and arms flailing in protest against the vast silk handkerchief which would be tied over my shrieking mouth to protect the tender ears of grown-ups. But perhaps the fault was not all mine. She had been my father's Nanny too, and, so my mother told me in after years, could never quite forgive me for being a girl. Also she may have needed to lick something since in her youth her young man had vanished to America and had never been heard of again. I do not think she was unkind to me, but she did not encourage what she called Namby-Pambyness. Nor, in his very different way, did our devoted father. He was our God as well as our father, tall, handsome, impersonally just and a famous cricketer. When he smiled his delightful smile and said 'Not bad,' (it was not necessary to add, 'for a girl') our young hearts swelled like Christmas balloons. He took for granted that Fusses are Never Made, and this, together with Nanny's disapproval of Namby-Pambyness, made us take stoicism as a Law of Nature, so much so that my young sister once walked for miles uncomplaining while an upthrust shoe nail bored a hole in her foot, and I said nothing when a table crashed on mine with such force that on going to bed I found a toe-nail adrift in my sock.

Our mother would have died for us, but to confide in her was out of the question. We sensed that she was frightened of Nanny, if we ailed she got really anxious, and there was also a second Law that she must *never* be worried. We were told that in her youth some doctor had diagnosed—I suspect erroneously—that she 'had a heart'.

A third Law in our upright and ordered world was 'Black is Black and White is White'. Any grey between was not envisaged. This Law held in the books which penetrated our nurseries and schoolrooms, and even when I reached the stage of novel reading. Fortunately, in the end Good Whites always triumphed over Bad Blacks, and the novels also informed me that all earthly troubles ceased with the ringing of marriage bells. These two dicta took a good deal of unlearning; and the process might have been disastrous had I not later on been fortunate enough to marry an extremely long-suffering husband.

A fourth Law was 'Little Girls must not ask Why?' This was very frustrating as I seemed to have been born with that bad word on my lips. I was also born lacking the love for dolls, needles and thread which all nice little girls were assumed to feel as a matter of course. What I felt, on the contrary, especially after I had learnt to read, was, 'Why waste time sewing silly petticoats for the silly creatures when a book could open the door on to splendid worlds filled with Knights, Genies, Mohicans, Treasure Islands and Black Panthers? And why, anyway, mustn't little girls ask why?' I never could get a sensible answer to that. All the grown-ups said, as they also said later of much that to me seemed harmless, was 'Because it's not done, dear.' Then why not, I thought, do what's not done, just to see what would happen? Possibly this almost obsessive desire to try the unknown could also be conducive to E S P. I remember, about the age of eight, standing in front of some Zulu spears which ornamented a staircase wall and were, so a grown-up had told me, poisoned, and debating whether to prick my finger on one of them to check that intriguing statement. But if it were true I should be dead and then I would not know the answer. Maddening as ignorance was, I decided in its favour.

Since questions were not in order, whenever possible one had —one just *had*—to try and find out for oneself. And thus, eventually, I found a use for a doll. Church bored me horribly. I wanted to run about, and the choir sent knives right through me by singing out of tune, but one Sunday my attention was caught by another intriguing statement, that worms could destroy dead bodies. I had wept over a dead rabbit and recoiled, feeling sick, from a dead hen, which had been mauled by a fox and was horribly smeared by its own eggs; but how could tiny soft worms, which did not seem to have any teeth, chew up even their fur and feathers, much less the huge hard bodies of grown-ups? (In those days women in English country houses were all firmly encased in whalebone.) But—if one buried that new doll with its silly flapping eyelids, that would give the worms a chance to show what they could do! The result of this exciting experiment was negative. After a restless week, exhumation disclosed that they had done nothing at all, and so I learnt that a statement made in Church could be inaccurate. I also learnt, though being very sensible people my parents did not say much, that it was not really done to turn smart new dolls into mildewy wrecks in attempts to test the truth of Holy Scripture.

It was at about the age of five, when I heard Fairy Stories for the first time, that I began to realize the awful hidden dangers that menaced us children. Of course one could never be so namby-pamby as to ask grown-ups for protection from them, and yet how readily, how gladly, I know too late, our parents would have given it. As it was, they seemed quite unaware that the more predatory inhabitants of Fairyland, about whom they so kindly read to us, did not obey the rules and remain there, but that every night after dark their sinister powers were unleashed in our world too. Almost worse, there was the Tiger which hung on the staircase wall. Every evening after tea my young sister and I were scrubbed, brushed and buttoned into white muslin frocks with blue sashes, and then sent down to spend an hour in the drawing-room with our parents. This would have been delightful but for the fact that to reach the drawing-room we had to run the gauntlet of the Tiger's snarling fangs, which hung at the most convenient height to crunch off our heads; and however safe a haven was Daddy's knee, there was always the awful knowledge that the only way back to the nursery was past those fangs again. In bed, after Nanny had put out the light and gone down to supper, things went from bad to worse. Quavering maa-maa-maaaas from the fields beyond the croquet lawn warned me that the Big Bad Wolf had arrived in search of his supper. Oh, poor, poor little lambs! And oh, would the one he chose be plump enough to satisfy his ruthless hunger, or would those slavering jaws come thrusting through the nursery window, agape for me? I knew I was marked for his own, for some kind grown-up had given me a 'lovely little Red Riding Hood cloak, darling', to wear when out for a walk.

After the Wolf there always came the Witch, tramp, tramp, tramping up the stairs, her eyes like angry stars under her high black hat. It was many years before I realized that her relentless footsteps had been the beating of my own scared heart. (I was careful not to feed my own children too young on fairy stories, but it did no good. My younger son tells me that his heartbeats became soldiers tramping down the street intent to kill.) Finally, and worst of all, night after night my sister's high chair transformed itself into a devil, which pursued me across the vast expanse of nursery floor—and caught me! At that moment, nightly, I died of terror, to wake up, shivering but silent, for Nanny did not care for being disturbed. I do not think I was consciously frightened of her, indeed, I thought I loved her, but it may be that those night-riding demons were in part symbols of her august displeasure.

I travelled, then, between two worlds, one of fairies and

witches, wolves and demons, the other of parents, grandparents, and nannies, rice pudding, horses and dogs. I was devoted to a brown retriever, Rover, whose liver doubtless made him touchy owing to a life tied up as guard-dog in the stable yard. My whole family were dog-lovers in a big way, but that this was cruelty never occurred to them. Perhaps Rover was one of the lower classes. He was very rude indeed to odd-smelling people called tramps ('Come away, dear, that's not a nice man') but he treated the hens and me with extreme graciousness and allowed us to share his kennel if we felt inclined.

Another thing that grown-ups did not appear to know was that some people had nasty Insides. Fortunately, extreme nastiness was rare, though some Insides, especially our gouty grandfather's if his mountainous white foot was knocked by mistake, would go off with a slightly unnerving bang. But he wasn't *nasty*. In fact, when, during the plum-tart season, he spluttered and swished *The Times* at marauding wasps, we could not control our mirth, and our poor mother, biting her lips, would mutter, 'Children, be quiet!' and quickly banish us from the dining-room to simmer down. It never occurred to us that she was battling against laughter too. But a few people had Insides which made me want to run away and be sick. The worst of these was a parlourmaid whom my innocent mother held in high esteem. She had cold, opaque, brown eyes and a mouth like a bilious cod, and I did what I could to get rid of her, even to pouring a bucketful of water from an upper window on to her smartly-capped head. This failed in its object. All it achieved was to earn me an afternoon locked in the box room to meditate on my sins. In the end the parlourmaid vanished rather quickly, her nastiness having, I supposed, at last become apparent to grown-ups. Nothing, of course, was said to us children and nobody related that nastiness to my own bad behaviour. Years later I watched my two-year-old son, who normally looked on all the world as his friend, behave in the same atrocious manner as I had done. An elderly cousin came to tea, bringing him a superb toy motor car, but he thrust it away and shrieked until she departed, muttering thoroughly justified comments on my bad bringing-up of the young. 'Why were you so unkind to Cousin Mary?' I asked when he was cosily having his bath.

He wrinkled his brow and for a time was silent. Then, 'She was *dirty!*' he said. I knew what he meant. Life had gone badly with her. She had married the wrong man and he had been morbidly jealous of her children. The boy could not have chosen a more apt word for her lonely, sad, disillusioned, embittered Inside.

But there was one person of whom I was not aware, either inside or out, and this seemed odd for my mother read to us about Him and prayed to Him every morning, and the whole household, except Alice, the cook, visited Him every Sunday. His name was God, He lived in the sky, He had made me and everyone else and He kept an eye on all of us all the time. Moreover, He could do anything whatever He liked. That being so, it seemed a pity that He had not made me good like my young sister, who did not have unpopular ideas but was quite content to ride a hobby horse or play with the dogs or a ball all day. My mother assured me lovingly that, if I prayed to Him, He would help me to improve, but for a long time, in spite of all my prayers, He gave no sign of His existence and I did not improve at all. However, one day after a bout of special wickedness, in despair I prayed 'fit to bust', as Nanny would have put it, and then for one ecstatic moment I found myself caught up into a warm and shining world where I was no longer a Naughty Girl, and there was no need at all to cry. But He did not keep me there and He never did it again, so I grew bored with prayers, particularly those in a little pink book with a white vellum spine from which, kneeling at her bedside, our devoted mother read to us every morning. Each prayer was preceded by an uplifting remark and one morning that was, 'Example is better than precept'. This was a chance to escape the book that was not to be missed, so I proposed to her that if she just set her children the example she need no longer bother to read them the precepts. (Years later her third much younger daughter asked her why she alone had been deprived of the lovely readings from the little pink book.)

So there it was, neither prayers, nor example, nor spankings made me a Good Girl. (When the spankings were administered by my mother she said to me pitifully, 'This hurts me more than it hurts you, darling', and a good thing too, I thought.) But there was always one ray of hope: grown-ups seemed to have no trouble at all in being quite perfect and they were always saying how fast I grew. Perhaps one far-off day I too would achieve grown-uphood and then, O bliss, O rapture, I would never again even *want* to be anything but Good.

Security was our mother's watchword. 'Don't climb trees, darling, it isn't safe.' 'No, darling, it isn't safe to swim.' So I dared not hope that adventure would ever come nearer than at second-hand in books. But when I was eleven the glorious impossible happened: our father was sent to India to reorganize its geographical survey and he decided to take his family with him. Like cumulus, stupendous visions billowed inside my head: Whales, Mountains, Elephants, Parrots, Maharajahs, Palms! Eventually all these wonders did materialize, though for the most part on the far side of an invisible security curtain. In our Calcutta garden, for instance, there waved palms just like those which supplied the Elephant's Child with bananas.

'Can we explore the garden, please?'

'No, dear, there might be snakes.'

A tarantula on the stairs was some consolation, so was a banded krait on the Maidan, but it was almost more than human nature could bear when a lovely Maharanee in a glittering saree asked if we children could visit her, and the answer was, No.

Sometimes, however, reality brushed our shoulders. During the hot weather the family migrated up the Himalayas to Darjeeling, and there romantic pedlars from Tibet appeared on the doorstep, followed by porters staggering under enormous packs, exactly as in the Arabian Nights. I spent blissful hours trying to paint them in their funny turned-up hats and smelly bulging garments. One pedlar had a particularly endearing grin on his yellow Mongoloid face and as a great treat I was sometimes given a few rupees to play at bargaining with him for little bronze dragon candlesticks and lumps of turquoise and Chinese porcelain spoons. One day he handed me a wonder straight from Aladdin's cave, a circular ivory bowl, thickly studded with red and blue stones embedded in gold scrolls and patterns. Enchanted, I turned it round and round . . . but . . . what ivory could take that bulky circular shape? Even elephants' tusks were long and slender. At last I recognized poor Yorick and nearly dropped him, for death by now had become a frightening thing. But training held. Fear must not be shown. I handed him back politely with regrets that I could not afford so fine a curio.

We children had never seen a mountain before. Now, right at our feet, rivers of billowing treetops poured down to steamy subtropical valleys miles and miles below, and beyond them the mountains climbed again, ridge after ridge, until they were lost in a blue and dreamlike nothingness.

'Look, children, there are the Snows,' said our father, pointing we thought towards the nothingness. For a long time we could not see them. We had not looked high enough. Then at last, towering against the cobalt sky, we saw Kanchenjunga, white, shining, inviolate, all but the highest mountain in the world. I could not—and cannot—formulate what moved me almost beyond bearing in the Hills. It was as if some wind of the spirit blew down on the childish creature and touched something in it awake, so that it could never be quite so childish again. One night after our return to England when our mother came as usual to kiss me good night, I had not been quick enough to dry the nostalgic tears from my face. 'What's the matter, darling?'

'Nothing, nothing at all.'

'But there must be something!' She looked hurt.

'It's leaving the Hills,' I mumbled and, as I had foreseen, her look changed to one of bewilderment. What could there be to regret in that land of dirt and disease and thieves and heathen ways? Some years ago I went to an international dinner party in Eaton Square expecting witty, pleasant talk but not 'real communication'. I found myself sitting next to an explorer who had just returned from Tibet and to him, surprisingly, I also found myself daring to mutter a little of what as a child the Hills had meant to me. After a pause he said the two words that of all others I would have chosen to hear. They were 'Those Presences!'

It was soon after our return from India—I was just thirteen—that I realized that in some intangible way I was at times aware of lesser presences in certain places. Some were grim and sad and I felt that if only I could *see* them they would be less unnerving. One was in my bedroom in my grandfather's house which overlooked Dartmoor. By day it was a gay little room, facing south, with a wall-paper festooned with blue ribbons and pink roses. But at night it was a very different place. Then a mysterious invisible Somebody shared it with me—and I didn't know who that Somebody was! Because of its presence I undressed in the nursery, leapt blindly from the door into bed, pulled the blankets over my head and kept well under them until a friendly housemaid flung open the curtains to the blessed morning sun. Had the Somebody been mentionable to a grown-up I might have learnt that my mother and aunt had both independently seen the apparition of an old woman standing at the foot of the bed, but, needless to say, they both kept this to themselves until years later after my grandfather's death. I suppose they assumed that children were not aware of what I am sure they called 'these things'.[1]

I also felt invisible presences in another aunt's house in Norfolk—melancholy frightening presences—but again, not until I was grown-up did I learn that to her they were not invisible, but she often saw them and took them in her stride. Years later I was told—too late to check it with her—that soon after her marriage she was lunching the other side of the county and saw a portrait of a man in seventeenth century clothes.

'Why,' she exclaimed, surprised into an indiscretion, 'that's the man who is always trying to stop me going upstairs at home.'

'That,' said her host, 'was Oliver Cromwell as a young man. As it happens when he was young he was involved in an unfortunate love affair with a girl who lived in your house.'

It is hard to get the emphasis right when writing of childhood experiences, and if I have painted myself as a quiet dreamy little girl I have got it wrong. Anything to do with Insides and Presences I kept carefully to myself, or rather, it did not occur to me to mention them, and on the surface I delighted in games and adventures just as much as in drawing, music and books. I suspect that I was also tiresomely observant, to judge by the caricatures of wives of Empire Builders in India which I found in an old drawing book the other day. They gave point to remarks made by an exasperated Nanny, 'If you're as sharp as that you'll cut off your own nose,' or—this one always fascinated me—'Teach your grandmother to suck eggs!'

[1] Since this book went to press I have heard, quite by chance, that there was a tradition in the village that someone had been walled-up in that room. Whether or not that was so, the idea might have been picked up telepathically from the villagers.

CHAPTER V

Growing Pains

My father wisely decreed that for the two years we were to be in India I need have no schooling, but could send for any books I liked from the Calcutta Club. The child was too young, he said, for them to do her harm. This enabled me to gulp down a very mixed diet of books with the indiscriminating joy that a mastiff gulps down meat, and the Indian servant who fetched and carried them got quite a lot of exercise. At thirteen I was sent back to England to live with an adored uncle and aunt and be instructed, along with their sixteen year old daughter, by a very Parisian governess. She instructed us in anatomy with the aid of the chicken carcase we had met at luncheon, and we had quite hard work to persuade her that the chicken's head had not been attached to its tail end. But I learnt some French.

My cousin I humbly revered, not only for her great age but because of her prowess at tennis, climbing trees and handling spirited horses. In lessons she had just been promoted to something called geometry, of which I had never heard, and instead of learning my history dates I listened enthralled while the governess tried to expound to her a delightful puzzle called the Pythagorean theorem. And I saw, I *saw* what it was getting at! 'Please, may I learn that too?' I burst out at last.

'No,' said the governess coldly, 'you are too young,' and later my cousin conveyed subtly that it was not done to be too much interested in that sort of thing. I felt ashamed.

That summer we went to stay in Winchester for the Eton match, and in my bedroom there I found a book called *John Inglesant*. I took in little of it, but it aroused the same unformulated, nostalgic delight that the Hills had done. Inglesant was clearly on a quest which made the adventures of Crusoe and Gulliver seem suburban. It would have been wonderful to ask a grown-up what it was all about; but I heard one of them describe young Humphrey Sumner (later to be Warden of All Souls) in a pitying voice as 'clever', and I feared that the book, *John Ingle-sant*, was 'clever' too. Better keep quiet about it.

Unexpected things now began to trigger off a kind of turbulent inner response. A harebell once did it, swinging by its invisible stalk with a grace that hurt on a bank in the New Forest—I suddenly saw it as beauty incarnate—and so, more and more, did music. (From the age of eight I had been trying to express the Music of the Spheres in a big way on a small piano, but the result disgusted me.) Unfortunately no such response was triggered off in church, where I was taken every week to bow the knee to God. But the trouble was I could not find Him to bow to. I could not even feel suitable misery when I had to recite, at what seemed interminable length, that I was a miserable sinner. And then, at last, came the solemn day of Confirmation. Now perhaps, I thought, when the Bishop lays his hand upon my head, he will turn me into a Good Girl, as the Fairy turned the Beast into a Prince. But, alas, no such miracle occurred, and at the end of the service I felt as flat as a punctured tyre. Had I committed the sin against the Holy Ghost and was my ultimate destiny the flames of hell? If only I could find out what that sin was. But obviously it would not be 'done' to ask about anything so awful. Oh, well, the flames of hell seemed a long way off. Let's think of something else.

The truth was, I was bored. In the secure and conventional country life of a far from well-off family, there was little to stimulate an over-curious child. But when I was fifteen and a half, adventure once more beckoned. My father was sent to run the Geographical Section of the War Office and the family moved to London, which to me was a Mecca, swarming with artists, musicians, writers and romantic Ruritanian foreigners. That my family would be unlikely to gravitate to such exotic individuals did not occur to me, and my dazzling visions seemed about to come true when my parents decided that I had had all the general education that a girl could need, and told me that they would provide a Bechstein—with their narrow means a most generous gesture— if I wished to concentrate on learning the piano. Did Christian wish to enter Paradise?

What I thought were the Gates of Paradise were the grimy doors of 194 Cromwell Road, and behind them sat a fat and red-faced archangel, the well-known pianist, Mathilde Verne, who had been a pupil of Clara Schumann's and in her youth had actually played to Brahms. Unfortunately for her own pupils she enjoyed playing on their nerves as much as she did on the piano, and by a velvety finger-tip touch of approval she would sweep them up to the skies, just for the fun, apparently, of casting them thence with a crash into the nethermost pit. Here my early training came in useful. I was cowering in the pit one day when she remarked reflectively, 'You know, you are the only pupil I have never managed to make cry.'

I shall die before you do, I thought. But why should anyone want to make anyone cry? Nevertheless she did open to us the minor heaven of chamber music where isolated young creatures could play themselves into a joyful unity. Here, at last, were moments of real communication.

It was perhaps due to the stimulus of extreme panic that at the age of seventeen I experienced the inner linkage of joint performance in visual terms. Mathilde never did things by halves and to launch the child prodigy, Solomon, she took the Queen's Hall and engaged Nikisch, no less, to conduct. And then, to show what she could make of even sub-human material, she decreed that amateur pupils should play a Mozart concerto for two pianos. I arrived for the one rehearsal under Nikisch just in time to see her turn purple, tear at her curly black hair and shriek, 'My God! I forgot to tell him there were amateurs playing. He will refuse to conduct!'

Even his kindly message that he too was an amateur did not prevent my knees from playing the drum on the underside of the piano keyboard until, on looking up to begin, I saw miraculously stretched from him to every player, including me, a shining cord. Owing to my cord something not me played with zest and assurance and entirely out of my class. At the end he bent down and clapped and said, 'Bravo! Bravo!' But I knew dimly, though he did not seem to, that he was congratulating himself, not me.

From now on the turmoil of adolescence in a creature totally ignorant of both psychology and physiology made me hell, merry hell, not only to my parents but to myself. Even the joy of music turned to inchoate longing for I knew not what, and to wake up in the morning from vanished celestial mansions to the muddy swamp of this 'solitude called life' became intolerable. Even to listen to footsteps walking down the street at night would drive me crazy. 'What's the point,' I asked my bewildered mother, 'of all this talk about sisters and cousins and aunts and cricket, of keeping bedroom drawers tidy and mending underclothes with invisible stitches?'

She tried pathetically to explain that nice girls liked their clothes and drawers to be in applepie order, to which I replied that clearly I was not a nice girl. She tried again. In her youth she had not only done, she had thought what her mother wanted, because she loved her.

'I love you too,' I replied, 'but I don't order my thoughts. They come. And I still want to know why mending petticoats is more worth while than practising Bach?'

'Well, music *is* only entertainment, isn't it,' she said, more puzzled than ever. I froze. We were a million miles apart. And I also felt painfully guilty at being so unlike my revered cousin, who was just the kind of daughter my mother, I felt, ought to have had. Her hair stayed tidy after strenuous sets of tennis, she never asked tiresome questions and she always said the right thing. Also her values were not like mine, cockeye. 'He doesn't hunt, he doesn't shoot, he doesn't fish,' she was once heard to remark of a rising young diplomat, now one of Her Majesty's most polished representatives. 'It's really quite uncouth.'

Not that my own parents disapproved, in principle, of things of the mind—my father even read Tennyson and Browning—but such things did not seem to have any connection with real life. I began to read Browning too and got quite a kick out of the fact that his wife, Elizabeth, and my grandfather were first cousins. It was exciting to have a run-away poetess in the family. But I got no change when trying to coax romantic titbits out of my tiny lace-capped Irish grandmother about the time she and grandpapa had spent with the Brownings in Florence. 'I was very fond of Baa,' she said. 'You never could have told she was "clever". But Robert *would* stand on the hearthrug and *talk!*'

So, then, the harder my inner whirlpool boiled, the harder I had to sit on its lid. And now, to the unconscious hunger for mental stimulus and for that mysterious Central Something was added the ferment of unrecognized sex. In my world such a word was obviously taboo, and I doubt if I had ever heard it. My nearest approach was to read in books about an idyllic affair called Love, which parfit gentle knights conducted with small and extremely beautiful lily maids. That it had anything physical about it, except perhaps a respectful kiss, I had no idea and I did not suppose it could ever come the way of gawky great girls like myself.

Soon after my seventeenth birthday my parents sent me to visit an aunt, and while with her, as a preliminary sortie into grown-uphood, I was to stay up to dinner, and play tennis and croquet with some 'nice' young men. I did not meet the young men in an auspicious mood. As there was no maid available to accompany me on the visit, my mother decided, after much anxious thought, that if I were taken to the station and placed in a carriage marked 'Ladies Only' and a tip were given to the guard, I could come to no harm on the journey. 'What kind of harm could I come to?' I asked, intrigued, but this question was ignored.

On reaching the station the maid went to buy my ticket and I took the chance to skip across to the bookstall. Lying on it was a small green book called *The Riddle of the Universe*. It was by somebody called Ernst Haeckel, price one shilling. *That* was what I wanted! And by good luck I had a shilling. There was just time to buy the book and slip it under my coat before being placed in the 'Ladies Only' carriage, where I could read it safe from interruption or inquiry. My poor mother! No bomb could have smashed more effectively the framework on which she had so carefully moulded her daughter's life. Here at last was the truth. There was no God. Beauty was a snare and a delusion, which merely served to conceal that the universe was a soulless mechanism, clanking round and round for ever and ever to no purpose at all. That night I stared at the stars from my bedroom window and could almost hear their rusty gearwheels creaking. Gone was any hope of finding that Central Something, and—my all-wise parents lived in a fool's paradise!

There was no one, of course, to whom I could possibly speak of this appalling discovery, so I hid *The Riddle* among my underclothes, shyly played the prescribed croquet and tennis with equally shy young men, said 'Thank you very much' to my aunt and returned home. To the embarrassment of the maid who was sent to meet me at Charing Cross, I was sick on the station platform and then retired to bed, bright yellow with jaundice. Why the child got it, no one could think. She was always fed on the simplest food.

On recovery I refused flatly to play anything but Bach fugues and the only thing I would read was an old copy of Bloxham's chemistry, of which I understood practically nothing. Fortunately the family didn't appear to notice anything odd; and, terrible as it was to be deceitful, I could not bring myself to tell them about the book or that the light that guided their lives was a will o' the wisp.

However, the young and healthy are very resilient, and whether or not there was any point in the universe, after a few months my little whirlpool gave an occasional gurgle. It was now, my parents decided, time for me to 'come out'. In other words, my hair would be done up in puffs and rolls, three feathers would be planted in it and I would be taken to bow the knee before my monarch. That this tribal initiation would change me, in the twinkling of an eye, into a grown-up as wise, balanced, decorous and kind as my parents I took for granted, and it was a shock to find that after it I was as unworthy a daughter and as much hell as before. The young men I now met at balls provided a second shock. They would all, I had assumed, be brilliant and witty and would dance like swallows, but, on the contrary, they appeared distressingly earthbound. Most of them stepped, rather painfully, on my toes, and their talk, what there was of it, seemed limited to cricket or killing things. Even the few who doubtless dreamt high dreams in the heavenly courts of Oxford did not, it was soon apparent, expect mere girls to intrude on these. One morning after a dance, I was playing clock golf with a good-looking undergraduate, and a spray of golden Virginia creeper twined itself round his ball. 'Trailing clouds of glory,' he muttered, absently, to which rather obvious tag, enchanted, I replied with another. At this he appeared to suffer from shock. 'You don't mean to say *you* recognized that?' he said, looking down at me with wrinkled brow. I blushed for shame.

My father's best friend was a general whose post was at Woolwich, and in July 1914 my parents took me to stay with him for a Tattoo. The place was full of splendid, vigorous young men who rode horses and hit balls with tremendous *élan*. With them I thought it wise to confine my remarks to 'Yes!' and 'How interesting!' and 'Not really!', and this went pretty well if they spoke first. But they usually did not. However, I admired them respectfully when they gaily took part in the mock battles of the Tattoo against the kind of enemy with which the British army had to deal— Boers, or Pathans or something, away in the far corners of the world. A few months later most of them were dead.

CHAPTER VI

Hunch and Healing

I cannot tell whether the incidents recorded in this chapter involved any faculty akin to E S P on my part, though the first two in hospital suggest that it may have been exercised by two sick people. That my actions in a number of difficult situations were more intelligent than my ignorant childish conscious self could initiate, I have little doubt. If so, they may illustrate that on such occasions I tapped something superior to that self, something which may either have been extra-personal, as when I was apparently lifted out of my class by inner contact with Nikisch, or personal, in which case it may suggest, as on a higher level creative inspiration seems to do, that some hidden side of a human being can be of finer quality than the conscious mind. The impulses to constructive action which seemed to be out of my class I shall label Orders—for want of a better word—but by this I mean no more than that they were confident and not initiated by my conscious self. Like E S P-type experiences, they emerged unexpectedly out of the blue.

To me the 1914 war came as a thunderbolt out of a clear sky. Hitherto I had taken little notice of politics, assuming that they were matters to be left to clever men. Anyway, my simple schooling had conveyed that the world in which we lived, a world of boring security guaranteed by the perfect and all-powerful British Empire, would last for ever, and it never occurred to my father to mention serious matters to his daughters. His War Office job, however, had in fact been largely one of preparing for the war that was now upon us, and he had exceeded instructions by printing maps ready for the unthinkable circumstance of a retreat by the British army from the northern frontier of France. But he had not been able to get his maps indexed, and at the outbreak of war his whole staff was whipped away. So he had to fall back on his children. My sister and I and our friends started the war by racing ahead of the retreat from Mons, square by square, on the maps he gave us to index on the dining-room table. I found this task fearful and wonderful. To make a mistake might, I felt, kill many men. And yet at last we were doing something real, something worth while.

My father soon acquired a more potent assistant, a young man he found wandering in the corridor outside his room in the War Office.

'Can I help you?' he said with his usual kindness and the young man answered sadly that they wouldn't have him in the army, he was too short.

'Come into my office and we shall see what you know,' said my father, and what he knew caused him to be taken on in that office from that moment.

So impressed was he with his new acquisition that he actually talked about him at home and in such rapturous terms that we labelled him Daddy's Pet. The Pet stirred up my rather subdued little whirlpool with talk of desert journeys and Bedouin and digs at Carchemish, but, oddly enough, I think it was when he told me about a Persian carpet in his possession, which was dyed with lapis lazuli to a blue so deep that it shimmered up into the air, that the whirlpool became a geyser. 'I will, I *will* get out of this cocoon,' I vowed to myself. Such a reaction was perhaps understandable for the Pet was T. E. Lawrence.

It having occurred to me that I could and would get out, a way turned up quite soon, but it was the last I should have chosen, an appeal in *The Times* for voluntary nurses, as the professionals were too few to cope with rising casualties. I was appalled, for my world went green at the sight of a cut finger, and I was sick at the smell of vomit. My parents were appalled too. 'You're far too young, you've led far too sheltered a life!'

But they had long since provided me with a trump card. 'Everyone knows,' I said, 'that girls are of less value than boys, and Johnny and Tommy were only eighteen and they are dead.'

The casualty lists grew longer and longer and at last they let me go—without a maid—for an interview with the matron at Barts. 'What reason,' inquired that starchy potentate, 'has a child like you to think she would be any use?'

'None,' I quavered, 'but you could always kick me out.'

On my second day at Barts the sister gave me a lamp to hold for a first dressing after a thigh amputation. Layer after crimson layer was stripped off and at last the spongy mess was laid bare. The patient shrieked, and I found myself in the kitchen with my head between my knees. The Matron had been right. I wished I were dead. Then came the Staff Nurse's voice, blessedly indifferent. 'Don't worry, Nurse. People usually do that the first time.'

She too was right. That patient's shriek, not curtseying in feathers, had been my initiation into something approaching grown-uphood, for now, for the first time I think, I learnt to look at other human beings, the patients, as themselves and not solely in relation to ME. I fell in love with the lot of them, their courage, their childlike simplicity, their sense of fun. One plump creature, who had lost both legs, gave me most gay and helpful instructions when I was promoted to doing his dressings, and when he was convalescent he discovered that he could elicit roars of laughter from his fellow patients by bouncing up and down the ward on his back side. I soon found I could sense and ease their physical aches and pains, but their mental processes were often beyond me. One cheerful boy confided to me in a hoarse whisper that he was only sixteen. 'Far too young to be fighting,' I said, priggishly. He wagged two fat pink paws in my face. 'Oi've killed *four* on 'em with these two 'ands, meself,' he said with no trace of emotion except annoyance at my stupidity. It was quite a change from home.

After three months at Barts I was drafted to Milbank Military Hospital, and was at once put on night duty to care for a Sister who had meningitis. As for most of the time she lay unconscious I took the chance, crouched in a dimly lit corner, to read *The Brothers Karamazov*. All went well until I reached the argument between the sick man, Ivan, and the Devil, at which point, to my horror, she leapt up, pointed a trembling finger at the foot of the bed and addressed the Devil herself. Very startled, I flung down the book and ran over to her, whereupon, to my great relief, she fell back unconscious once more. I knew nothing about telepathy but it seemed clear enough that in such situations one's mind should be kept on milder topics than devils, so rather shakily I decided to write a letter to my young sister about a new spring hat. That, fortunately, aroused no response from the sick nurse.

This incident shook me and there was no one to whom I could mention it. Nor could I bring myself to go on reading the book.

Even when asked to do so last year (1960) I found it an effort and when I reached the crucial passage was astonished to discover that now my only reaction was compassion for the morbid fantasies of a sick man. Why, then, had the Sister chosen to indulge in E S P at that particular point? One explanation suggests itself. On her deathbed in 1946 my mother spoke as if her whole life had been haunted by the fear of going to hell—so there were things she could not say either!—and when young I could perhaps subconsciously have picked this up. On the surface too I had come to assume that my own wickedness condemned me to the same fate; so possibly an early fear which I had repressed may have provided the stimulus for the sick woman's E S P.

A few weeks later I was set to watch a man who was gravely ill and delirious after a severe operation. He appeared quite unconscious of my presence, and I felt desperate because there seemed no way to reach and comfort him. This desperation may perhaps have enabled a confident inner Order to emerge to consciousness. The Order was 'Think him quiet.' I was much surprised but remembered the sick Sister and tried to obey, and, to my even greater surprise, he at once fell into a quiet sleep. Naturally enough, in view of my raw ignorance, a little later the Staff Nurse moved the screens to see how he was doing, and woke him up. I was able to think him asleep again, but soon afterwards the Ward Sister came rustling in and woke him once more. I tried a third time, but it did not work. Then, suddenly, the tossing and delirium ceased, he looked at me with quiet, rational eyes— he was obviously an educated man—and said calmly, 'It's no use concentrating any longer, Nurse. I shall not be going to sleep again.' Then the rational man vanished and the agonizing delirium began once more. If this is how death comes, I thought, it is even more terrible than I had imagined. But suddenly his face lit up. 'It's Annie!' he cried, gazing in joyous recognition at someone I could not see, 'And John! . . . Oh, the Light! . . . The Light! . . .'

Soon afterwards he died. I was impressed by the fact that so soon after he had appeared to be aware of my thoughts he also appeared aware of invisible presences. Could they, I wondered, in some unknown sense be 'real'? In the light of *The Riddle* it seemed almost inconceivable; but still I could not be sure that they were only created by his fevered imagination.

These two incidents gave me some slight confidence that lack of surface communication with the patients did not mean that they were of necessity beyond the reach of comfort and we V.A.D.s needed all the confidence we could get, for to some of the trained Sisters we were clearly refuse the cat would not have stooped to bring in, and we also at times had to cope with situations far beyond our knowledge. But from now on Orders were inclined to take these over. We used, for instance, to be left at nights for long periods in charge of badly wounded men, with no Sister or doctor at hand, and without authority to give sedatives. 'Make your own sedative,' said Orders one difficult night. 'And make it nasty.'

I knew nothing of suggestion but I obediently made a revolting concoction of drops of the nastiest medicines in the cupboard, plus a spoonful of salt. This, to my great joy, gave excellent nights to officers and men alike, until one evening a highly intelligent undergraduate, whose appalling neck-wound forced him to sit up night and day with his head slewed painfully sideways, not only failed to respond to my miracle drug, but said peevishly that he did not believe there was anything in the stuff. This threatened my whole régime; so, drawing myself up with the air of an outraged matron—I was beginning to learn the value of cap and apron—I said I was NOT accustomed to being called a liar, but in view of the exceptionally trying nature of his wound I would for once strengthen the dose. A second even more disgusting variant of the same concoction had him asleep within ten minutes, and he did not wake up till morning, when I heard him telling his neighbour that he had not believed a drug existed that could have put him to sleep the night before.

This and other successes encouraged Orders, and they now began to deal with minds as well as bodies. A badly wounded young creature was tying himself into knots of gloom, and for him they prescribed a poem. 'Tell him to be that silly cow swishing her tail in the lily pool,' they said. That cow was the heroine of a poem by T. E. Brown (the Victorian 'My Garden is a lovesome spot, God wot' poet). I rushed home on my half-day off duty, fetched a fat volume of his effusions, dumped it on the gloomy one's bed table, and said with authority: 'Stop moping and be that cow.'

Next day he greeted me quite cheerfully and said, 'I am that cow, and I feel better.' I met him again as a stranger thirty years later at a gilded party. He was now an elder statesman, but not one, I felt, to be reminded that in his storm-tossed youth he had been a cow.

The next two incidents are not concerned with E S P, but they may be relevant as they illustrate the extent to which one facet of a personality can repress another. I thought that my new impersonal Nurse self had replaced the old over-reactive ME. I now learnt that ME was still going strong and that Nurse was merely sitting on a lid. Queen Alexandra had given a piano to Milbank for the Officers' wards (the men already had one), and the Matron decreed that after supper I could entertain the patients on it. Soulful Chopin was popular, and one evening I was dishing out the soulfulness with a tablespoon when an S.O.S. came from the men's hospital for a spare V.A.D. to help with an emergency operation.

Since dealing with patients from the Mediterranean theatre of war, whose suppurating wounds had not been dressed for weeks, I had been conceited enough to think that I had learnt to 'take' anything. But not, I now discovered, as dessert after Chopin. The man to be operated on was a drunkard; drunkards bleed like pigs. 'Count the swabs inside him, Nurse.'

One, two, three, four, five . . . Oh, God, I'm going to faint, have I kept track, what splendid ferocious words that surgeon knows. . . . I can't. . . . 'Yes, sir, there were eight, they're all out.' Was that cold calm impersonal voice actually *mine*? . . . How neatly he sews. Queer that revolting lump of flesh will be a person tomorrow. What is a person? . . .

And who, I thought, later, would be an artist, as hypersensitive all the time as I had been made for a moment by a dose of Chopin?

Ashamed at this narrow escape from disgracing myself I battened down the lid more firmly; and, I discovered many years later, quite efficiently. In the spring of 1917 Milbank buzzed with rumours that a draft of nurses was to be sent to Macedonia. Olympus! Centaurs! The Argonauts! Socrates! Alexander! Winged feet took me to the Matron's Office and in my excitement I addressed her as if she were merely human. 'Oh, Matron, I know I'm not senior enough, but please, *please*, put my name down on the list for Salonica.'

To my astounded delight she picked up a pen and did so then and there. I did not tell my horrified parents how my name had got on the list—the first time, apart from hiding *The Riddle*, that I had had the strength of mind to keep any action of mine from them.

Eventually a snail-like train trundled the nursing staff for two camp hospitals through war-racked France to Marseilles, and from there half of us soon set forth in a troopship for Salonica. They returned two days later subdued and oddly clothed. A U-boat had got the ship and, to our shame, few but the women had been saved. The rest of us were sent on the next ship and we had a hilarious voyage. The men taught us 'Ousy-ousy' and we grumbled when called away from it in haste to the boats. The whole thing, we said, was 'such fun'.

For me the end of that little story came in 1934. My husband and I were taking our children to America, and we thought that being so young they had better do boat drill. Quite unexpectedly —we were all laughing together on the boat deck—a wave of panic broke over me, so acute that, muttering some lame excuse, I fled to our stateroom to face it alone. There, jittering with terror, I learnt that beneath the surface I had not really thought the voyage to Salonica such fun after all.

For our hospital, the Q.M.G. in Macedonia had chosen a plateau site halfway up Mount Hortiach, thinking that, being high, dry and windswept, it would be more or less mosquito-free. But the mosquitoes thought otherwise and, no one knew why, we soon held the record for malaria of any hospital in the command. Round us the mountains exuded a brooding sadness and past and present seemed to co-exist. Across the bay towered Mount Olympus, and a mile down the valley thin and hungry refugees from Asia Minor threshed their meagre corn with half-starved oxen, just as their ancestors had done in Old Testament days. When quarrels flared up they brought the loser in for us to mend, and to me their outlook was a new one. The assailant of one man came to inquire tenderly for his health. 'Why did you bash his head in if you feel so friendly?' we asked, intrigued.

'I wanted his hen,' he said, 'and now I've got it. So why should I bear him ill-will?'

Our hospital was a dysentery centre; but an enemy almost as grim as that dreary disease was boredom—the boredom of long weeks of convalescence, made slower by the malaria which blanched the men's blood to water, and unbroken by games, gramophones, books or visitors. Even the food was vitamin-free and tasteless, and there was nothing to look at but the barren hills. More than medicine, a nurse had to purvey comfort, to greet each man in the morning and tuck him up at night as if he were the only apple of her eye. One night in the rush of settling in a convoy—a hundred-odd desperately sick men straight from the line, to one orderly and two bedpans—I forgot a semi-convalescent patient until, at 3 a.m., my lantern caught the flicker of his lonely eyes. 'A rigor again?' I whispered.

'No, Sister, but you didn't say good night. How could I go to sleep?'

Sometimes Orders created problems for me. A nice boy was dying of blackwater fever, about which in those days practically nothing was known. One night five doctors clustered round his bed, and when they left the senior among them said to me, 'You can do what you like, Nurse. We can do nothing more.'

I felt helpless and desperate, but Orders did not hesitate. 'Ask him what he wants more than anything in the world.' I knelt down, took his fingers in mine and did so. His answer—I could hardly hear it—was 'A red rose, Sister'.

'You shall have one tomorrow,' I heard myself saying, 'I promise.'

Had I been mad? What miracle could produce red roses on those arid hills? But the miracle had been prepared by destiny. The hospital despatch rider had been a patient in my ward and I happened to know the Quartermaster General. So the despatch rider added to his mail for G.H.Q. a shameless S.O.S. 'Please, somehow, get a red rose *at once*, or one of my men will die.'

In a few hours he rode up the mountain again with a miraculous bunch of roses which the Q.M.G. had obtained from the garden of a Greek magnate. They were scented like an English garden and almost as black as night. When I went on duty the boy was still just alive. I held them under his nose. 'Here are your roses. Smell them.'

He half opened his eyes, almost smiled, and—against all reason —he got well.

But Orders were not always so novelettish. One man was dying because he would not take nourishment. 'It's no good telling me to use my will,' he muttered, 'I have no will. I became a drug addict in Persia. I tell you, I'm going to die.'

'Nag him,' said Orders. 'Nag! Nag! NAG!' This was entirely contrary to my instinctive approach to a sick man, but I obeyed. At last he wailed, 'Oh, I'll eat anything, anything, if you'll only go away!'

In three weeks he was eating hospital stew as if he liked it.

There were sometimes quiet nights when I had time to wonder about human nature as I crept from tent to tent. Never having heard of Freud or Jung or the subconscious, the questions that puzzled me had little to feed on in my ignorant head. Where was the consciousness of sleeping or delirious men? Far away, or in abeyance? There were occasional hints that something was continuous. Three weeks before he died one man, a Scot, left us mentally, crying out that he had to look for a saxpence in the left hand corner of the worrld. But just before he died 'he' came back and looked at me with affectionate rational eyes. 'Ye're a good gurrl, Nurse,' he said.

I nearly burst into tears, for suddenly I knew without a doubt that some part of him had been aware all the time that we were trying our best to care for him. But I did not know what happened to him when he left us. Had he snuffed out for good? Was it pure sentimentality, or could it conceivably please him, if I took time off from the living to prepare his body for the grave?

In Macedonia I had a stroke of luck. For the first time I met someone far more knowledgeable and intelligent than myself who was actually willing to talk to me about such problems. This was Vivian Usborne, the Senior Naval Officer—though he was not so senior in years, being the youngest and, it was said, the gayest Captain in the Navy. He talked a little of the Society for Psychical Research, but I took for granted that this was a body far too remote and august for such as I; it was only twenty-one years later, in 1938, that I found that ordinary people were allowed to join it.

Later still, soon after the Second World War, Vivian died and I had an experience which I do not know how to interpret. He appeared to return from his last voyage to tell me that the conclusion he and I had finally come to, that death was the end was quite mistaken. But that incident belongs further on in Chapter XIV.

In September 1918 I learnt a little at first hand about alterations of consciousness, for I achieved temporary fame by surviving a sharper attack of malignant malaria than anyone else had been known to do, and it gave me some knowledge of the morbid hallucinations of disease. In my case, at least, the ghastly gorilla-like devils that leered at me out of an immense gold embossed Victorian frame, which hung mysteriously in the air without any support at the foot of my bed, were quite unlike the hallucinations which I later experienced spontaneously or under mescalin.

I crawled back to work in time for the final push and its successors, the armistice and Spanish 'flu. Staff was so short that I was alone in charge of a whole block of tents, and on going on duty on armistice morning I found that all the 'flu patients who could stand were celebrating in the tents of the dysentery patients who could not. 'Now they'll give each other their beastly bugs,' I thought morosely. But joy was more potent than bacilli. Nobody gave anybody anything. I was able to take a useful part in the celebration, for during the morning a kind friend at G.H.Q. sent me a miraculously procured bottle of champagne, and one hundred and eighteen carefully measured teaspoonsful enabled all my patients to drink to Peace and a World Fit for Heroes to Live In. We believed with childlike faith that we should go home to such a world.

I have recorded here a few samples of the Orders which came into my head in relation to healing. There were fewer later on in private life, perhaps because, if anyone fell ill, competent experts were there to turn to. But they did occur, and when, on one occasion, I was acutely anxious about my elder child, they contradicted the diagnosis made by an expert in a fashion that appeared to hint at E S P. I record that incident in Chapter XII, together with Orders of other kinds.

CHAPTER VII

Interlude

It was fairly easy to feel detached when describing a remote child-hood and youth and a nurse's relations with her patients. But now, for the short period between demobilization and marriage, an absurdly self-centred Me re-emerged, about whom it does not encourage my self-esteem to write. Thanks to Orders I had done quite well as a nurse; but on reaching home the nurse vanished— I even reverted to being sick when my mother's bulldog was sick on the floor—and, like an emotional adolescent, I continued to over-react to everything. 'You're a skin short,' people laughed at me. But being a skin short may be symptomatic of a temperament prone to E S P-type experiences, and as certain emotional crises seemed to evoke them, I ought perhaps to try and summarize this boring period before turning to my main E S P-type material.

It was raining cats and dogs when, early in 1919, I arrived home in London. My loving family welcomed me with arms wide open; but to me—it was quite unjustified—they seemed to be living in a goldfish bowl, cut off from the real world where men and women could be cruel and unjust, where love stories did not always end 'happy ever after' and where the sick could die because those car-ing for them did not care enough. The gulf between my family and me widened when I discovered that in Macedonia I had not been as invisible as, being the youngest and humblest of V.A.D.s, I had unthinkingly assumed. Exaggerated rumour had reached home about the innocent safety valves by which my two particular friends and I had sought, when off-duty, to forget the sadness of the wards. We had gone riding over the mountains with gay young officers, knowing very well that V.A.D.s were not allowed to ride. We had slipped across the Aegean in a torpedo boat and climbed quite a way up Olympus on the backs of strong-minded mules. And I, with a young archaeologist, had climbed up the dome of Salonica Cathedral and taken photographs while clinging like a monkey to the Cross at the top. Though we did not know it, these childish escapades had caused a good deal of amusement in the Command and had earned us the indulgent nickname of The Three Disgraces: but though my parents were sensible people and said very little, I did not feel that such behaviour really accorded with their orderly outlook.

Unfortunately rumour had also linked with mine the name of one of our escorts—in most places outside the hospital barbed wire we had to have escorts, by order, on account of brigands— and unfortunately rumour was right. Purple mountains and blue seas and orange sunsets, iris and asphodel and oleander, set against a background of war, pestilence and death, could end for the young in one thing only—romance. Early in 1918 I dived into my first love as a dolphin dives into the sea, with, though I had no idea of it, a HERO I had myself invented, all-wise, all-beautiful and all-entertaining. The young man I cast for this exacting role was a French officer of Scottish descent who was doing liaison work with the British. All would have been well but for the fact that he was an idealist and that his Catholic family had married him off to the daughter of a neighbouring landowner just as the war began. This and my Puritan upbringing drove us to behave with a frustrating virtue which may have led to my first exterior visual hallucination, apart from the morbid fantasies induced by malaria.

In September 1918 Alex was sent on a mission to Paris, and on waking one morning after he had gone I saw him, just for a fleeting moment, standing in bright daylight in the entrance to my tent. A little later the same thing happened in reverse. He wrote to me from Paris that I had come into his room, sat down at his side and taken his hand. As is frequent in such cases, I was in no way startled or even surprised at my hallucination. Nor, which is far more odd, was Alex at his, though he was a shrewd and incisive soldier who would have laughed in theory at the idea of anything so absurd as E S P. Yet he reported my appearance in Paris when he knew I was in Macedonia as a plain statement of fact. 'You,' he wrote, 'were here.'

There is no evidence, of course, that I was there. A more plausible explanation is that both his hallucination and mine were self-created. But why did we create them? Was it merely frustration, or was this the only way that our conscious minds could be told of subconscious telepathic interaction between us?

The end of this ordinary little romance is short. I knew very well that, the circumstances being what they were, for Alex's sake I would have to break away. But to do so seemed like putting an end to one's life somewhat early, for my mother had always taught us that nobody could love more than once. And I thought I loved Alex. But she did not. 'It's impossible,' she cried. 'You can't! He's married!'

I had acquired compassion for patients but not for parents. 'If one did achieve the impossible,' I asked cruelly, 'would you think divorce or murder the greater crime?'

'Divorce,' she said, in tears, and once more I withdrew into my egocentric self and shut the door.

Fairly soon Alex and I did the only thing our outsize consciences made possible. We broke apart. (He was killed in the Second World War, but I had no awareness of it.) After the break I was too busy wallowing in my own selfish misery to notice the miseries of other people, but from this bout of egoism I was rescued by the care-free giggles and romps of some very young debs at a dance . . . (Might as well dance. What else was there to do?) Silly creatures! What did they know about life? And—what on earth was I doing cavorting about in silks and satins when the men I had nursed and loved had come back to unemployment and despair and hunger, instead of the world fit for heroes to live in, to which I had so hopefully drunk with them?

Shame landed me in a London University Course for Social Workers. Its students had to spend half their time gaining practical experience, and to do this I was sent to a branch of the Charity Organization Society in the East End. It was good to meet the men again, but I was appalled at the conditions in which I found them. The C.O.S. personnel were painfully competent and, according to their lights, kind and well-meaning; but my ears went back at their calm assumption that—provided the recipient was Moral and Deserving—the Almighty had empowered them to dole out as charity (horrible debasement of a beautiful word) the succour which I felt to be Everyman's due from his fellows as a matter of course. So, as usual, I found myself lined up with the Bad instead of the Good. One of my friends was a scally-wag of an ex-seaman who told me splendid Münchhausen stories over the counter of his extremely smelly fish-and-chip shop. One day, in a burst of good fellowship, he even offered to teach me jiu-jitsu —I should find it useful, he said—but I had at least grown up enough to realize that the C.O.S. could not be expected to stand for that, even in their most junior representative. As it was I mutinied because the elderly Committee jibbed at providing irons for the seaman's skinny crippled little daughter, on the ground that her subnormal mother had run away with another man. 'Would you have found that a sufficient reason,' I asked, 'had the crippled legs been yours?'

This was impertinent, but it got the irons; and at the end of the course they offered me a permanent job. I refused it, explaining as politely as I could that all I appeared to have done when working for them was to wangle help for the sick which they should have had by right and to deprive Jones of a job by getting it for Smith. Did the whole system, perhaps, need altering rather than patching up? They looked pained and said good-bye, I am sure with relief.

I was still naïve enough to get a violent shock at the terrible plight of so many of my fellow countrymen; and yet more naïve in believing that among the thousands of Great Writings by Great Men which I found on the shelves of the College library some would expound how such wrongs could be put right. The library had the effect on me that the smell of fish has on a kitten, and I read voraciously far more than I could digest. 'Education,' said my coach austerely, 'does not consist in gobbling facts but in trying to exercise your judgment about them. Try yours on this.'

This was J. S. Mill's *Essay on Liberty*. That evening I scurried home from the C.O.S., rolled myself in a rug in my unheated bedroom and exercised my judgment till the sun rose. I ended frozen and in tears. The argument was doubtless as clear as daylight; but, try as I would, there was one place where I could not make it follow. Evidently my father's dictum that women had no judgment had been a just one after all. But when next day I abjectly confessed to failure, my coach replied peacefully, 'Of course you couldn't make it follow at that point. It doesn't.'

It will be hard for the sophisticated to believe that I was still so naïve that a cosh between the eyes could not have knocked me out more neatly. If a mere girl could detect a flaw in a Great Man's argument—then, obviously, Reason would have to go the same way as Religion. Life was no more than a quicksand. *Nothing* could be trusted. However, this shocking discovery gave a fillip to my own little critical faculty, which was usually smothered under respectful hero-worship, and I began to doubt whether the Socialist Utopia, so enticingly preached by my coach and the good-looking G. D. H. Cole, was more desirable than the Establishment upheld by my family and the C.O.S. Were the working men I knew, lovable as they might be, much more intelligent or disinterested than my parents? And would they relish being pushed and shoved into doing just what the Webbs thought good for them? As for me—this horrifying thought came into focus gradually—was the only way to avoid doing actual harm to do nothing at all until at last I died?

I should not have included this childish episode but for the fact that in the end it too ministered to my ferret-like urge to find out something more about the real nature of human beings. How could anyone help anyone, if they didn't know what kind of animal they were trying to help? To begin with, however, my loss of faith in the various efforts to benefit mankind which I had recently seen in action induced a kind of numbed passivity which must have made me worse hell than usual for my long-suffering family to live with. I took for granted that this passive mood would last for life, but one afternoon, about a year after Alex had said good-bye to me, I was shaken into a turmoil by the sudden conviction that he, although invisible, was standing in front of me—just there, quite close! A few days later I heard that he had come over to the French Embassy on a two-day job and on that afternoon had been asking mutual friends for news of me. 'I'm not dead yet,' I thought morosely, and redoubled the killing-off process. This progressed according to plan for another year, and then, when dining out, I met a brisk young British officer, whom I had run into three or four times in Macedonia, and who had been very kind to me. Dysentery and malaria had hit him hard, and on our way home from dinner the friend with whom I was staying remarked casually, 'Well, he looked a pretty scarecrow, didn't he!'

I stared at her in astonishment. 'You wouldn't talk like that if you knew I was going to marry him,' I thought.

As so often happens with E S P-type experiences, this flash of knowledge was not at all startling. On the contrary it seemed as normal and inevitable as the fact that on the morrow the sun would rise. But next morning it had submerged again; and I did not remember it until, to my extreme surprise, three months later we were engaged. To my equal surprise and immense delight, I found that although one facet of my prospective husband was a competent young soldier who had been nominated to the Staff College for good work during the war, another facet indulged, as I did, in flashes of apparent E S P. And, marvel of marvels, he did not think them odd. He told me that he had had such a flash about me even before he knew I existed, and that when we met in Macedonia, and I had, it appeared, been argumentative, he had thought with amusement, 'Little do you know, my girl, that you are going to marry me.' But he too had temporarily forgotten these flashes, and again like me, had had a romance elsewhere.[1]

The brisk young soldier did marry me, and thereafter until shortly before the Second World War the ordinary wife and mother kept her foot on the head of the inquiring ferret—but only just, and it often snapped and bit. For long periods too the search for some 'swift and unimaginable byeway' towards that elusive Centre was more than half forgotten in my care—absurdly exaggerated—for husband and children. And my sporadic E S P-type experiences flickered up mainly, though not exclusively, in relation to them.

[1] Many years later I had a similar apparently precognitive flash which pinpointed exactly the girl our son was going to marry. I had never heard of her, but they met and married about a year later.

PART III

Personal Experiences

CHAPTER VIII

Classifying My Experiences

So much, then, for the triple background to my experiences—the mental climate, E S P in general, and my own personal past. Against it I now had to take a fresh look at the experiences themselves, and the more I looked at them, the less I liked them. Some, most embarrassingly, could well be acclaimed by the most ardent Believers as 'Voices from behind the Veil!' Others were vague as last year's dreams and most were trivial beyond belief. It was very tempting to scrap the lot as being due to chance, inference or expectation, or even, as a masterful great aunt of mine would doubtless have said with a contemptuous wave of her lorgnettes, to 'pure imagination, my dear child, pure imagination!'

Yet a part of me felt sure that they were not due to any of these things. And once again some chance comments came to my aid. The first of these was by Sir George Thomson. 'It is the greatest discovery in method that science has made that the apparently trivial, the merely curious, may be clues to the understanding of the deepest principles of Nature.'[1] The next courage-giving remark, as once before, was by Sir Julian Huxley. 'We must follow up all clues to the existence of untapped possibilities like extra-sensory perception. They may prove to be as important and extraordinary as the once unsuspected electrical possibilities of matter.'[2]

I should perhaps apologize for harping on my own inhibitions. I do so because they emphasize the unnaturalness of the mental climate vis-à-vis E S P, which, like the air we breathe, is otherwise liable to go unnoticed. If it could be studied with the same dispassion as, say, the neutrino, the day might sooner come when it would either be accepted as a natural process or disproved. In either case, a great deal of fraud and superstition on the one hand,

[1] Sir George Thomson, F.R.S. *The Inspiration of Science* (O.U.P., 1961), p. 2.
[2] Sir Julian Huxley, article on *The Destiny of Man* in *The Sunday Times* for September 7th, 1958.

and the unwholesome bottling-up of what may be a genuine capacity on the other, would be discouraged.

My experiences divide roughly into two kinds: a passive awareness, usually fleeting and on the fringe of the mind, of apparent presences or of situations not perceptible *via* the senses; and an inner prompting to action or comment on behalf of other people, which seems either beyond my normal capacity, or absurd in the light of facts known to me at the time, but turns out to be relevant in the light of other facts learnt later on. As I said earlier, for want of a better word I have called these promptings Orders, though I do not thereby want to suggest that they must come from outside myself. I do not know where they come from, except that it is not my conscious self.

Some of my experiences were unverifiable and could well be labelled fantasy, but others corresponded with the thoughts or feelings of other people, and a very few with events that had not yet taken place. At first it seemed best to record them in chronological order, and thus indicate trends; but when I tried to do so, there were no trends; the experiences varied according to circumstances. Moreover, if listed chronologically they would be no more than a patternless string of anecdotes—and anecdotes by the dozen are an excellent soporific. Yet it is still by the dozen that they are needed in a field-naturalist's search for clues as to process, agency, motivation, encouraging or inhibiting conditions—in fact for anything which might suggest an experimental situation in which ESP might be coaxed to appear to order. It seemed then a better plan to group the experiences into classes. But this also created a difficulty: most experiences fall into two or more. A telepathic signal, for instance, can emerge to consciousness as a waking exterior hallucination, a sensation, an inner voice or image, a dream, a scent, or a simple urge to action (as when I telephoned to Victoria Station 'because I had to', without knowing why). Nor was it always possible to decide whether an impression was telepathic or precognitive, or even whether a simple impulse to action beyond my conscious capacity might not after all be due to no more than subconscious inference or to a bit of information read long before and then forgotten. However, in the end I have followed this plan more or less, apart from the next two chapters. The first of these contains a mixed group of experiences which I record together because they all appeared to follow on my marriage. The second describes the apparent effect on my embryo E S P of some unusual acquaintances.

Another problem was how to intersperse experiences and comment. No-one wants a mountain of comment about a molehill of experience, yet strings of experiences without comment may not reveal their possible significance. Here too I have tried to compromise by keeping comment down to begin with and increasing it as there was more material to consider.

The externals of my adult personal life are much less significant in the context of this book than the childhood and adolescence that have already been described. Nonetheless they may have some bearing as an indication of whether the general background to an experience was stimulating or peaceful, anxious or secure and stable. To make that background more coherent I append, merely for reference if needed, an outline of the main changes in my outward environment from my marriage until today.

1921   Marriage. Husband at Staff College.

1923–4 Husband at War Office. Quiet Life.

1925   Birth of first child. I suffer from 'theories' about the need for mothers to look after their own children and carry them out.

1927   Move to the country when husband returns to his regiment.

1928   Birth of second son. Stay with Gilbert Murrays, when husband sent to Turkey as Military Attaché. Worldly life begins when I join him there.

1929   Husband transferred to Brussels and The Hague.

1931   As Army promotion blocked, husband transfers to Foreign Service. Posted to Berne.

1933   Posted to Budapest.

1934   Posted to Washington.

1938   On being asked to run the exports of a friend's firm, husband leaves the Foreign Service and returns to England. I join the Society for Psychical Research.

1939   Tour Africa. War. Husband returns to the Army. I am

involved in W.V.S. work, etc., mainly at home in the country, to a small extent in London.

1943   Take a house in London.

1948   Difficult period. Private income fades away. Country home sold. In London husband and sons start to build up a business based on machines designed by themselves. In time left over from domestic chores I also start to build up a life along the lines of my own interests.

1953   onwards. Seeds sown begin to sprout.

CHAPTER IX

Marriage and ESP

In 1959 my husband engaged a new secretary, a brisk and sensible girl. One morning soon afterwards when busy typing, I felt an urge to run upstairs and speak to him, although I had no reason to do so and wanted to get on with my work. As I walked into his study I heard him say to the secretary, 'I told you so.'

'Told her what?' I asked.

He laughed. 'That you'd come if I called you mentally,' he said. I glanced at the girl. Her eyes were round with shock. What sort of employer had she come to—Aleister Crowley?

This little incident, like my husband's summons to meet him on his return from the Second World War, was a typical example of the many correspondences between my reactions and his situation, or *vice versa*, which had long since convinced us that some sort of subconscious extra-sensory linkage existed between us. We should not, of course, expect them to convince an outside investigator, for he could dismiss each one separately as a chance coincidence, or as the result of expectation, since, as Professor Broad has pointed out, the very unexpected seldom happens. And no investigator could feel the force of the impulse which drove us to the action desired by the other, or even be sure that we were not responding to imaginary appeals.

The interest, if any, of the correspondences which I shall give lies, not in their mainly trivial content, but in the possible implication that my husband and I are in subconscious telepathic contact with each other. And if us, then surely others; we are not exceptional people. It may be then that even if signs of it never emerge to consciousness—or at least are never recognized—many other married couples, parents and children, teachers and pupils, and co-enthusiasts or co-workers, are also linked beneath the surface in a similar fashion. If so, John's reactions to James or Jane, which seem exaggerated or illogical in relation to their overt behaviour, may be due in part to the subconscious impact of their hidden attitudes towards him, whether of love or hate, admiration or envy, compassion, indifference or scorn.

Because it seems possible that the mutual impact of my husband's marked personality and my own, which was very different, may have stimulated our embryonic E S P, I will begin by trying to sketch our early surface reactions to each other as I saw them.

In me marriage soon melted the frozen coma induced by the preceding years of frustration and disillusion, but my grandiose adolescent ideas of Service to Mankind and the Search for the Ultimate were now for the time replaced by positively ferocious service to my new and delightfully immediate Godlet. Fortunately for me—and for him—he quite liked being served, and as he had just been sent to the Staff College I also obtained thereby some mental nourishment. To begin with I was allowed to type his essays and to draw maps and plans of battles. On one of my maps his mentor wrote, 'Just what Nap would have liked,' and my cup was full. Then one glorious day my Godlet threw down before me some enormous tomes on Nap's strategy and said, 'Read these and see if I am interested.' My cup ran over.

This sort of thing was scarcely my natural diet, but it taught me two very useful lessons. One was that if you did not say exactly what you meant the worst could happen—even to tangling up at a cross roads two divisions on the march. This struck deep, for I pictured the result as much like a skein of wool on which a kitten had been at work. The second lesson was the old Staff College maxim: 'There are four courses open to the enemy. He will always take the fifth.' In other words, keep a look out for possibilities beyond the obvious ones.

For our first summer vacation we planned to drive down through the apple orchards of Normandy to stay with my Godlet's uncle amid the vineyards of Anjou. As usual I did an advance build-up of an ideal cloud-cuckoo land; Henri IV (*à la* Fred Terry) *Les Trois Mousquetaires*, Cyrano—Romance, Stimulus, Sparkle, Wit. . . . What I got was *La France Gastronomique*, *La Famille* and a mental Feather Bed.

In Anjou that year the weather was abnormally hot, and although the scent from the towering conifers cunningly grouped round the chateau was quite intoxicating, it was soporific as well. With the warmest generosity *la Famille* took me to their hearts—

was I not the young bride of 'notre cher cousin'? But they had come from Paris to relax, and relax they did. Moreover, as I soon discovered, it would never have occurred to the uncle, brilliantly intelligent as he was, to sparkle for the benefit of his own women-folk. Women, though useful after their fashion, were more or less ornaments, to be kept—very tenderly—in a glass case. Not that he had come to Anjou to provide mental stimulus even for men, but to enjoy in peace his beautiful garden, his superb wines and his exquisite sauce-drowned food. I found it hard to keep awake during the long hot ritual of meals and at one luncheon for a visit-ing prelate I was even driven to mutter the name Lloyd George to my neighbour. Nowadays that name stirs nobody's blood, but then it was guaranteed to give any Frenchman apoplexy. In a flash the whole table was ablaze, and I no longer had to rack my brains for something to say.

My husband, who had been working all out, naturally sank into this feather bed of family devotion and good living with a sigh of enjoyment. I thought that I too was enjoying myself, but in fact I grew a little bored and perhaps somewhat 'liverish'. This led to an odd experience, which, though unverifiable and not telepathic, may still be indicative of an E S P-prone temperament.

One hot night my husband was peacefully sleeping while I wriggled, restless and wide awake, at his side in the great carved bed. At last the excessive peace became unbearable. 'I can't stand it,' I thought, 'I shall wake him up to make love to me.'

Before I could carry out this egoistic idea I did something very odd—I split in two. One Me in its pink nightie continued to toss self-centredly against the embroidered pillows, but another, clad in a long, very white, hooded garment, was now standing, calm, immobile and impersonally outward-looking, at the foot of the bed. This White Me seemed just as actual as Pink Me and I was equally conscious in both places at the same time. I vividly re-member myself as White Me looking down and observing the carved end of the bed in front of me and also thinking what a silly fool Pink Me looked, tossing in that petulant way against the pil-lows. 'You're behaving disgracefully,' said White Me to Pink Me with cold contempt. 'Don't be so selfish, you know he's dog tired.'

Pink Me was a totally self-regarding little animal, entirely composed of 'appetites', and she cared not at all whether her unfortunate husband was tired or not. 'I shall do what I like,' she retorted furiously, 'and you can't stop me, you pious white prig!' She was particularly furious because she knew very well that White Me was the stronger and could stop her.

A moment or two later—I felt no transition—White Me was once more imprisoned with Pink Me in one body, and there they have dwelt as oil and water ever since. It is only quite lately that I have become aware, though I seldom remember it, that I can deliberately identify myself with White Me and watch without feeling them—that is the point—the desires and repulsions that must inevitably toss all Pink Mes around. If Freud ever struck such cases perhaps they helped to lead him towards the concepts of Id and Superego; but they seem to be rare, certainly more so than the experience of simply seeing one's double, as reported, for instance, by Goethe.[1] One point may be of psychological interest. On other occasions when I have been aware of duality in myself, the split seemed to be because a hidden part of me wanted to act on information which the conscious part did not possess. But here the wills of White Me and Pink Me were entirely opposed. I felt as Swedenborg once wrote: 'It was strange that I could be of two minds, quite separate at the same time.'

One of my adolescent illusions, fostered by Victorian novels and the harmonious lives of my parents, had been that with marriage came total companionship and agreement on every subject. But I had not reckoned with my own questioning, critical, rebellious temperament, so very unlike my mother's, and it did not turn out quite that way. My husband told me recently that it had been a bad shock to him to find that I would not take his word for things. At the same time I over-did the hero-worship, and he was patience itself while I slowly and reluctantly woke up

[1] I have only struck one other such case at first hand. A nice simple motherly woman told me spontaneously that she had split soon after the birth of her baby: one of her continued to lie in the bed while the other stood by its side. I asked her a few casual questions, among them, 'What did you both think of each other?' She replied at once with emphasis, 'The Me outside looked on the Me in bed with profound contempt devoid of all feeling.' This was exactly White Me's attitude to Pink Me and encouraged me to think that at least neither she nor I had invented our experiences, whatever had caused them.

to the fact that no one human being could have all the contradictory attributes, virtues and interests with which I insisted on crediting him. His way of dealing with me was just to go on quietly being himself and doing what did interest him. What emphatically did not was the verbal tennis which was my favourite sport, mainly, I think, because it gave me a flickering illusion of real communication. The result was that for about two years I treated him to a monologue, until one day, to my great surprise, I found I had run dry. An experiment seemed indicated; at luncheon I would not speak till he did. 'What's the matter?' he asked comfortably, peeling his apple after a silent meal.

'Nothing. But I've told you everything I've ever felt or done.'

'Oh, that's all right,' he said kindly, 'I like your babble.'

That was delightful to hear, but it did not replace the sense of communication given me by the to and fro of verbal tennis, and I now wonder if perhaps my life-long exaggerated need for communication, particularly with someone I adored, may have provided the emotional fuel which drove signs of our underground linkage up through the censorship to consciousness more often than with most other people. He too may have had a special need for oblique signs of companionship, for on the surface a far harder school than mine seemed to have conditioned him always to shelter behind silence and detachment. He had had two exuberant elder brothers, a broken home, a father subject to fits of rage, and, knowing little English, he had come late from France to an English School where he was laughed at for being a 'Froggie'. In his Paris school, on the contrary, he had been set upon as one of the wicked English who had burned *Jeanne d'Arc*.

Our surface interests, except for music, were different too. He did not share my passion to discover what made my fellow men tick, preferring to use his hands to make more docile machinery tick himself. Work apart, his hobbies were to invent gadgets, to tinker with cars in order to drive them faster than their makers had designed them to go, and to play golf. And yet, safely hidden behind this competent man of action I soon discovered a mystically minded intuitive, who took ESP in his stride and had no apparent wish to pester nature with petty questions merely because she did not always conform to Newtonian science. I well remember when first he told me of a hunch which saved his life.

He was working at a forward artillery observation post on a hill top which was being heavily bombarded. Nevertheless, he kept his companion on the job until, suddenly, he 'knew' that the moment had come. 'Now!' he cried. 'Drop everything and clear out.'

They just got away as a shell fell slap on the post. An investigator would have to say, 'Chance', but I knew what he meant by 'knowing'. So the story set me off once more on my usual stream of questions: How? Why? What is time? and so on. To a man of his intuitive-cum-practical temperament it must have seemed the twittering of a sparrow, and a tiresome sparrow at that. How tiresome I only realized forty years later when, as a joke, I told the family of my host's remark that I must have been hell as a child. 'Not half as hell as you were as a bride,' he broke in with feeling.

So much for background. I will now give a few illustrations of the type of correspondence which led us to suspect telepathic interaction between us. The most elementary correspondences were between my sensations and his—or his thoughts about them, I do not know which. This resembled Mrs Severn's impression that her lip was cut about the time her husband's lip was gashed by a tiller, and it was first brought to our notice in 1927 by an absurd incident in which my sensations corresponded with his thought. We were living in a romantic but chilly converted barn in a Sussex village, and my husband, having just been appointed Military Attaché in Turkey, was going regularly to London for Turkish lessons. One cold winter's day he said to a casual acquaintance in London that he could not get his feet warm. 'Oh, yes, you can,' said the man, 'Just concentrate on the idea that they are warm and they will become so.'

My husband was amused, but he will always try anything once and during the afternoon he concentrated diligently. It was to no avail. His feet remained as cold as ever. Those were the days before the blessed invention of fur-lined boots for women, and my feet used to feel like twin icicles when I took my small boy for walks on the freezing cliffs. But not so that afternoon. For no apparent reason they burnt like furnaces, and it was not until I heard my husband's joke about his abortive effort to warm his own feet that I wondered if he had succeeded with mine instead. (I always wish I knew whether mine really became hot or whether I only thought they did.)

Such correspondences have continued throughout the years, but obviously they can only be striking to other people if they occur when my husband's bodily or mental state changes suddenly and it is possible to check the correspondence in time. This will only happen very occasionally. It last did so in 1960. While getting the breakfast I unexpectedly felt so very ill and depleted that the idea struck me, 'Well, I'm growing old, perhaps I'm going to die.' Then I thought muzzily, 'At least I'd better try and get Frank's breakfast first,' and somehow carried on. A few minutes later my husband came down in his dressing gown, flopped on to a chair and confessed, rather shamefacedly, that he had nearly fainted as the result of too long and too hot a bath. He had never done this before.

Since I find the reactions of learned sceptics to ESP-type experiences instructive, I mentioned this one to an eminent friend of mine. 'It's obvious,' he said at once, 'that subconsciously you heard the gurgle of the water, noted that your husband was in his bath longer than usual, deduced that it had been too hot and then acted out his resultant faintness.'

He waved aside as irrelevant my feeble comments that my distant bedroom was two floors up from the bathroom, that I had come down from it after my husband had gone to the bath, and that he had not come down to breakfast later than usual; also that similar correspondences had occurred when we were many miles apart.

Now to turn to my husband. He does not appear to reproduce my bodily sensations, but with mental impressions the traffic between us is two-way; the difference being that he seems to respond to my wishes only if they are ardently directed towards him, whereas I may pick up his situation even when I am not at the time in his thoughts. The next two incidents illustrate this difference.

The background to the first is that in 1949 by a stroke of fate due to the war, our main source of income went down the drain, and I was flagging with worry and overwork. We had sold our house at Sunningdale but a friend had kindly lent us a cottage at Sunninghill, and one Friday night my husband went down there for a week-end's golf. I said I would join him on the Saturday afternoon as I had an appointment in the morning, but it fell through and I set off early instead. It was very hot and I felt exhausted and was in consequence unreasonably discouraged when, owing to an exhibition at Olympia, three successive Green Line buses arrived at Victoria unexpectedly full. After waiting in the hot sun for over an hour I took a bus by a circuitous route to Englefield Green, about four miles from the cottage. On getting out of it I thought I was going to faint, and stumbled, full of self pity, to a telephone kiosk by the roadside, hoping against hope that my husband had arranged to play golf in the afternoon and would be free to come and fetch me. When there was no reply to my call tears of fatigue began to trickle down my cheeks. Like a child I longed for his support and comfort. In fact, if E S P is encouraged by emotional fuel, on this very trivial occasion it was there in plenty.

Then my luck turned. A passing motorist kindly gave the drooping object a lift to the Sunninghill crossroads, five minutes' walk from the cottage, and as I got out of his car my husband drove up from Sunningdale.

'What an extraordinary coincidence,' I cried enraptured.

'It's not a coincidence,' he said. 'We played early and as we were walking in from our game I felt quite suddenly that you needed me, here, at once. I had just accepted a drink from my opponent, but I cried off, saying that after all I had to meet you.'

Two points about this incident may be worth noting: his impression was not in accord with rational inference, for there was not a bus from London at that hour in the morning, and anyway I had said I would come in the afternoon; and he went to the place where I was, rather than to where I had been when I longed for him to fetch me.

In contrast, here is a case where I responded to his annoyance over a minor mishap, although it was not one he had expected me to remedy. For a time during the 1939–45 war he was a Deputy Director at the War Office and he used to come home to Sunningdale to sleep whenever possible. One dark wet November evening my mother and I were sitting quietly together after tea and I broke the silence by saying, à propos of nothing, 'Frank has no torch. I must take him one to the station.'

My mother was not pleased; even in her old age she was full of fears for her children, though never for herself. 'He always takes a torch,' she protested. 'It's absurd to walk all that way in the rain for no reason at all.'

I did not want to annoy her; in fact, I found it hard to stand up to her; yet the conviction that my husband needed a torch to get home in the blackout was strong enough to make me brave her continued protests—and the weather—and walk to the station. It was worth it. On getting out of the train he exclaimed spontaneously, 'I am glad to see you. My torch gave out as I left the War Office and I wasn't at all looking forward to that long walk in the dark without one.'

I do not remember ever having taken such apparently irrational, not to say inconvenient, action when it was not needed.

I am tentatively inclined to suspect that when my husband's thoughts or feelings are not directed towards me, I do not become aware of them unless they are accompanied by a spurt of emotion, but that when they are, less emotional fuel is needed. By the time we were sent to Washington in 1934 my response to his wishes if they were directed towards me had become so commonplace that, since the Embassy staff were not encouraged to make outgoing calls, when he wanted to speak to me he sent me a mental message to telephone him. That, it will be noted, was a valid situation, and all went admirably until he began to talk about how well I responded. This gave me a reputation to keep up, I became self-conscious, and for a short time took to imagining that he wanted me when he did not. But that died down when I ceased to think about it.

I am sometimes able to ferret out objects which he has mislaid, but there is no means of knowing if this really goes beyond commonsense, plus experience of his habits. On the other hand, it may suggest that a bit of his own subconscious knowledge can on occasion emerge in me although it has been repressed in him. The other day, for instance, I found his income tax papers, for which he was looking everywhere, most improbably hidden away under his handkerchiefs in his chest of drawers.

Rational conviction that a thing cannot be so may also prevent the emergence of subconscious knowledge that it is so. In our youth my husband owned a fast motor cycle which, like all such vehicles in those days, seemed to enjoy conking out when most urgently needed. I knew nothing of its mechanism, but at one moment of crisis I said, pointing to the handlebar end of a cable which wandered thence mysteriously into its innards, 'Your trouble is at the other end of this.'

'That,' he said patiently, 'is the last place it could be.'

It was also the last place he looked an hour later—and there, indeed, was a most improbable trouble. It is conceivable that he was already aware of this subconsciously, and that it emerged in me because it could not break through his logical conviction that such a trouble was out of the question. But where motor-bikes were concerned I, unlike him, was quite untroubled by logic.

The natural reaction to this type of anecdotage is likely to be, 'Very well, if you think you have a permanent link with your husband, why not demonstrate it to order?' And the only answer I can give will seem foolishness to those who do not share this kind of experience. First, there seems to be a kind of complementarity between my conscious and my subconscious receiving level, with the result that conscious attention and effort inhibit the emergence of E S P-type impressions. So does anxiety to please, much as anxiety to win at tennis is inclined to make me play badly. Apparently I must feel carefree, and the impression must be unexpected, except on a very few unpremeditated occasions when something inside me has said, 'Now! Now's the moment; Try now.' But that may not happen for years at a time.

Another impediment to experimentation with my husband is that he would only undertake it dutifully to please me, and I would be aware all the time that he would far rather be doing something else; not a situation, as any experient will agree, which is likely to lead to success. In fact, it seems that for him, as for me, the situation usually needs to be a valid one—we must really *want* to communicate at moments when sensory methods of doing so are not available.

Postscript

A day or two after I had finished this chapter a trivial correspondence illustrated so neatly the pattern I have come to expect between my husband's thought and my action that I cannot resist adding it.

I was lunching out and expected as usual to prepare a meal

for my family before I left. (They almost always lunch together at home to discuss their joint work.) But at breakfast my husband said, 'You can have a treat today. No lunch. I shall be out and so will the boys.' It sounds exaggerated, but I could have shouted for joy. At about eleven o'clock, however, my typing was interrupted by the feeling that I must go at once and say to him that if he had changed his mind about going out, I could, of course, fix up something for him to eat. This irritated me. He had volunteered that he was lunching out. But I had to go. He was delighted. Within the last few minutes he had opened a letter telling him to expect an important telephone call at 1.30, and he was wondering if it would be too heartless of him to change his plans, stay at home, and ask for some food after all.

CHAPTER X

The Snob and the Cult

This chapter recounts a number of experiences connected with a new circle of acquaintances whom I met through a friend of my husband's. They took the idea of E S P in their stride, and although I jibbed at their somewhat soulful outlook, their attitude may have stimulated my own mild tendency towards E S P-type experience. No gift, especially a minor one, is fostered by unbelief. If his examiners were to inform a young pianist that 'We know you can't play the piano, you never have played the piano, and anyway, no such things as pianos exist', he would be unlikely to perform his best. But at least he would have sensory evidence that his piano did exist, whereas there is seldom confirmation that a fleeting impression may be extra-sensory until some time after it has occurred. Take the following incident when I lost £20 by lacking the courage to obey the urge to action which I call Orders, in the face of rational disapproval.

In July 1949 I was shutting up the house for a month, and Orders said that the water should be turned off at the main as a pipe in the attic bathroom was going to burst. I knew that this irrational prediction would stand little chance with my rational husband—it looked far more like fussing than E S P—and, as I expected, when I told him of it he kindly gave me the technical reasons why pipes did not burst in high summer. At this I decided on a fatuous compromise: I would leave the water turned on as he wished and take a key to our builder for use when the pipe did burst. Although he too explained that pipes never burst in the summer I just had the strength of mind to press the key into his reluctant hand, thank him, and fly. When the pipe did burst as Orders had warned me, his charge for repairing the damage was £20.

To revert to the Enthusiasts. I met them like this. During the 1914–18 war my husband was billeted for a time on a charming old lady, who petted him as old ladies love to pet agreeable young men. On being introduced to her I fell at her feet, a real tribute since she was a pillar of a Cult based on a popularized version of Oriental philosophy, and I had a prejudice against all Cults. Also I found the members of this one particularly trying, for they seemed to think they knew more about running the Cosmos than I did about darning socks. But my husband laughed at me. 'Don't be silly,' he said, 'these people are very kind. And you pretend to be interested in human nature. Why be snobbish about a new line on it?'

That remark struck home. They were very kind. And I liked snobs even less than Cults. Moreover, deep down there still lingered a pale little hope that since neither reason nor orthodox religion had proved a guide to that mythical Centre I never could quite forget, perhaps some day someone unorthodox might hint at a trail towards it. In fact, as regards the Cult, I was rather like one of Pavlov's dogs, not quite sure whether I was about to get a shock or a bone.

Through the old lady we met another Cultist, Mary, whom I liked and admired in spite of her odd beliefs and in spite too of her evident conviction that I belonged to a spiritual Lower Third, whereas my husband's consciousness was worthy to function with hers on a Higher Plane. Years later I met her again by chance, and she told me that she had had hard work to keep her end up in face of my arrogant disdain at all she valued, where as my husband, she said, had not despised her at all. Nor, as a matter of fact, had I. On the contrary I was impressed and intrigued by her casual exercise of E S P. (It was she who had sent us the list of houses at Wimbledon.) But I did not think her perfect, and I realized too late that with her it was not enough to conceal one's thoughts; one had to control them. My first intimation of that was absurdly trivial. I noticed one day that her petticoat was showing beneath her skirt, and wondered whether I knew her well enough to say so. 'Is it?' she said at once before I had spoken, 'I'll hitch it up.'

Mary's frequent E S P—which she used in a gentle unobtrusive way to help the sick—brought home to me that to square such a capacity with a Haeckel-type universe was about as easy as squaring the circle. Surely, there was something here crying out to be investigated—and seriously. But it did not occur to me that I could ever take the humblest part in anything so grand as serious investigation or even make contact with those who might undertake it. Still, I could watch quietly for hints and clues on my own.

I will give two examples of the kind of 'hit' I saw made by Mary, because her achievements in that line caused E S P to become a more vivid reality to me. It did seem too difficult to attribute them all to chance.

Soon after my husband had had a long and painful overhaul of his teeth by an extremely expensive continental dentist—one I had begged him not to stay with, incidentally, as I 'knew' he would do him harm—Mary said, pointing out an upper molar, 'You've got an incipient abscess in that tooth. I can see it coming in your etheric body.'

Etheric body! I winced. But my husband laughed. 'You're wrong this time,' he said. 'That tooth has just been passed by an expert dentist as perfect, and anyway I feel no pain.'

'Go and get an X-ray,' she retorted, and partly to prove her wrong, he did so. She won. Our own dentist complained indignantly that the extremely expensive dentist had made a bad mess of the tooth and there was an abscess beginning to form in it.

My second example concerns an entirely mental matter, the subject of a passage in Dean Inge's book on Plotinus which had been lent me by a friend. I had mentioned the book to no one, not even my husband, the lender did not know Mary, and she had not visited us since it had been in the house. It was far above my head and I did not get through it, but I did respond emotionally to a fine passage of which the general theme was intellectual love. Soon afterwards Mary sent me a message that she agreed with my comments on the bit about intellectual love in the book I was reading.

This was good, I thought, but I am ashamed to say that the snob in me did not care for the manner in which she claimed to have heard my comments. I had made them, she said, while our bodies were asleep and I was visiting her on the astral plane. I winced again.

It was many years before I realized the childishness of such snobbery, or that E S P, like information conveyed in dreams, is liable to take a dramatized or symbolic form which may seem actual to the experient or dreamer. Even if they do not exist, chakras, auras and etheric and astral bodies are apt enough images in terms of which to describe an experient's awareness of another person's thoughts or condition. Nor in those days had I realized that Cults may be havens for experients who have been treated as odd-men-out in the orthodox world. It must be a great comfort to live in a mental climate where one's experiences are looked on as normal, even if this does include etheric and astral planes. I still have to battle with snobbery to admit that, after all, these have not been disproved, and that my dismissal of them is suspiciously like the ardent Sceptic's dismissal of E S P; they offend my commonsense. (Was it Einstein who pointed out that commonsense is no more than a deposit of prejudices and that every new idea has to combat this accretion of 'self-evident' concepts?)

Whether it was merely through meeting Mary and her friends, who took such things for granted, or through a touch of subconscious jealousy and desire to compete, I cannot tell, but in the course of the next few years I indulged in three out-of-the-body type experiences myself. They taught me that such experiences seem as real at the time as Westminster Abbey or a piece of cheese. The first two were induced by music, one at a Queen's Hall concert, the next, surprisingly, in an hotel in Paris. On that second occasion we had come back from a New Year's dinner party, which in spite of good food and good friends, had seemed rather 'unreal', and on returning to our hotel I felt a shock of delight at hearing Chopin being played superbly in a nearby salon. I crept in. The pianist was alone and when he paused I said, greatly daring, 'Play me the G Minor Ballade.'

'No,' he replied, 'but I will play you the A flat.'

It was a beautiful performance, and when I had thanked him and returned to our room I lay down on the bed to mull it over. Almost at once the whole vivid soaring climax existed again, simultaneously, not in sound but to my inner eye in colour.[1] I was swept into it and up it until I emerged at the top into a vast and beautiful marble hall, oblong, with painted walls and the whole of the east end open to the night sky and the stars. While I was staring enthralled at these splendid surroundings my husband

---

[1] Galton's study of synaesthesia in normal persons is of interest in connection with this type of experience, which I also had under mescalin. See his paper 'Visions of Sane Persons', *Proceedings of the Royal Society*, 1882.

thought I looked odd and touched me gently. The effect of his touch was far from gentle: it forced me back sharply and painfully into my body (I naturally do not suggest that this is really what happened: it is what I experienced), and shaken and disappointed I told the poor man what I thought of him in no uncertain terms. At the Queen's Hall, too, he had thought I looked odd and had forced me back by a touch; but on that occasion I could not afterwards remember what I had experienced when I 'went out' on the music, beyond that it was glorious and that to be brought back so suddenly to 'this muddy vesture of decay' was acutely painful and disappointing.

My third excursion was not triggered off by music but by a thoroughly petty motive: mere curiosity. One of Mary's friends, whom we had come to like very much, had asked us to stay for the week-end, and he remarked at dinner that he and a group of friends practised meditation on agreed subjects, sometimes together but also separately every morning at eight o'clock. 'What will your subject be tomorrow?' I asked casually. He would not tell me. 'These things,' it appeared, were not for the uninitiate. At that, like an inquisitive child, I thought, 'Very well! I shall find out for myself.'

Next morning I got up early and at eight o'clock sat down on a hard little upright chair in the middle of my brightly lit room and prepared to 'listen in'. After a few moments I found myself in a serene and shining world of motionless peace, and there I could have stayed, calm and content, for ever. At the time I did not analyse it; I was just content to exist; but on looking back I see it could be described as a glorified version of a phase of going under an anaesthetic.[2]

The beautiful peace did not last long. It was soon shattered by agonizing thunderous bangs which crashed right through me. I tried to leap aside, and then came a very shaking experience. I had nothing with which to leap. No body. No edge. And nothing else had an edge. Yet all the time the terrible bangs went on.

[2] In the early 1930's I once, by way of experiment, enabled myself to go under very slowly by flipping away the anaesthetic several times with my hand, as if I did not know what I was doing. I watched sight, touch and hearing vanish, and then, before going under altogether, there was a moment of clear consciousness; but not consciousness of any objects.

Desperately I sought for an edge to something, somewhere. Then, suddenly, again without conscious transition, I found myself back in my body, shaken and furious. And the cruel bangs had turned into the mildest of taps on my door. (Ever since I have well understood why mediums, honest as well as fraudulent, can fear sudden noises and lights. In a state of dissociation these must be very trying.) I rushed to open the door and there was my husband, atrociously cheerful, to say that breakfast was ready.

'Why have you been battering down the house?' I exclaimed indignantly.

'But I only tapped very gently,' he replied with his usual patience.

At that I tore downstairs and flew at my host. 'What on earth have you been meditating about to knock me around like this?' I demanded—at the time I took for granted that he was the culprit—and at this unexpected Maenad attack the poor man gave up his little secret. 'I was only meditating on Unity,' he replied.

Really, I thought, how childish to conceal so harmless a topic, and I was about to dismiss the whole thing in a superior fashion when it struck me—Unity—and I had found myself in a world without an edge. Was there any connection? Later on I tried this on a psychologist, but he would have none of it. 'It's perfectly clear,' he said, 'that you fell asleep.'

Perhaps I did. But as the experient I know that I had had a good night and felt thoroughly awake and intrigued, and I cannot in honesty dismiss the alternative that I had telepathically picked up the idea of Unity and conveyed it to my conscious mind by 'living' it. That telepathy may have come into the experience was supported too by another hit, this time a direct one. Being amused at this curious new method of picking up information I thought I would try and look in again when our host went for his group meditation. This time I got the exact subject—a most unexpected one—not in any dramatic fashion, but verbally. Suddenly I felt ashamed. This was eavesdropping where I was not wanted. I did not try again.

Another new type of experience arose through a visit with Mary to a friend of hers, whose E S P, she said, was at least as good as her own. I was partly intrigued, partly reluctant, for from what I had heard I had snobbishly pictured the friend as a Holy Crank.

A huge fire made our host's room very hot, yet I refused to take off my heavy fur coat, an unconscious gesture, I expect, of dissociation from Holy Crankhood—and a silly one, for the friend turned out to be a gentle kindly man. However, keeping on my coat did draw my attention to an experience which otherwise I might have failed to notice. They gave me a chair by the fire, where for a time I sat quietly alone as everyone knew everyone else but me. Soon, to my surprise, I noticed that although I felt too hot I was also shivering. This did not make sense, especially as the shivering came from my middle, outward. At last it grew so violent that I exclaimed, involuntarily, 'I do wonder why I'm shaking like a jelly?'

'You're only reacting to the magnetized figure on the mantelpiece,' said my host, without surprise. At this, needless to say, I looked up as if stung, and there indeed was a little figure just above me which I had not noticed when I came in.

'Magnetized?' I asked puzzled, for to me the word conjured up magnets and bars of steel. But he meant something very different—that an object had been stepped up, so to speak, by means of a ritual, to 'radiate a Higher Vibration'. At this my snob's blood ran cold. And yet I had to be honest. I had reacted pretty strongly to something. (It occurred to me years later that I might have done so telepathically to my host's belief about the little figure.)

I fairly soon lost touch with my acquaintances in the Cult, for kind and interesting as some of them were, I was not open-minded enough to endure their belief that they knew so much about so much. All the same I owe them a debt of gratitude for awakening me to reactions which otherwise I might have ignored. To concentrate attention on outward things is a powerful instinct and it is easy to remain oblivious of these delicate intimations.

CHAPTER XI

Orders

'Freeing my mind of all thoughts of the problem, I walked briskly down the street, when suddenly at a definite spot which I could locate today—as if from the clear sky above me—an idea popped into my head as emphatically *as if a voice had shouted it.*'[1] That is a description by a scientist of how an intuitive idea came to him. He was wiser than I when a somewhat anti-E S P psychologist asked me to tell him how I received what I called Orders.

'Well,' I replied innocently, forgetting those precious words 'as if', 'I hear a voice . . .'

'Ah, a voice,' he broke in, and his own voice could not have said more clearly, 'Obviously an unbalanced type.' 'And this voice,' he went on, 'does it come from far or near or . . . ?'

'No, no,' I said hastily, trying to make myself clear, 'I don't mean I hear a voice . . . at least . . .'

It was hopeless. Our language is not designed to convey this sort of thing and sensory analogies are always misleading.

I could make Orders sound more respectable by calling them hunch or intuition, but I want to emphasize, as the scientist did in the above quotation, that they come out of the blue, sometimes 'as if' from another person and always as a surprise to the conscious mind. One has not wittingly thought it out, so to speak. Perhaps this kind of impression has something to do with the mechanism of the brain as a computer, but the experient is still faced with the fact that his computer's calculations occasionally seem to be based on facts with which it has never been fed.

For the most part my Orders prescribe action on behalf of my family, or, as in hospital, for someone for whom I am partly responsible; and it can be action which seems very odd at the time and only makes sense in the light of later information. When I

[1] My italics. Quoted by W. I. B. Beveridge in *The Art of Scientific Investigation* (Heinemann, 1951), p. 68.

am talking to a person who is 'in a mess' they can also prescribe comment which would be the last I should make by nature, but which also turns out to be useful. Occasionally they are not about mundane things. In 1938 when my husband left the Foreign Service for business, I found myself bereft of the dope of diplomatic life, with a reasonable income, the boys at school, and face to face with—myself. Myself was quite detestable and I was swept by shame and a longing for guidance as to how, instead of always drawing good things out of the pot, I could put a little something back. How, how to acquire a glimmering of wisdom? Dagger sharp and *de haut en bas* the answer came, very much as from someone else, inside my head: 'If you want to learn, don't buzz so. And don't ask so many questions, but sometimes listen to the answers.'

This kind of thing is naturally liable to be dismissed with a shake of the head as a sign of mental instability; but in my role of greylag goose, that is not my affair. Moreover, I have often found Orders useful, although they can also be trying when, in the light of what I know at the time, they seem to run counter to commonsense. Then the conscious mind resents them and will produce the silliest arguments to prevent them being carried out. I will give some instances.

The general background to the first instance is that for years I fussed too much about the best way to educate our children. Having been mad enough to bring them into this difficult world, I felt that the least we could do was to equip them to cope with it as well as possible. In other words, I stocked up emotional fuel for E S P. When the boys were very young I was still 'agin the Establishment' actively enough to be highly suspicious of the public schools of which my conventional relatives were the products; and my husband, with his usual tolerance, was quite happy to drive me round the country looking at various progressive institutions. But progressive institutions seemed to smell of Cult, and finally I succumbed to our friends' assurances that Eton could provide the best education for a boy who cared to learn—and also, I began to suspect, the best combination of freedom with responsibility. One of the friends was Sidney Webb—though he did specify 'in College' and he did add with a twinkle like the sun at noonday that no doubt I would be surprised to get such advice

from him and that a Quaker school was an equally good alternative. But we were not Quakers, and at last it was towards Eton
that I cast my eyes, only to be told, which I knew already, that
all the best houses had been fully booked for years. 'However,'
said one kindly Senior Tutor, 'at the last moment a vacancy in a
good house might crop up—but don't bank on it—it's most unlikely.'

I did not bank, but I hoped with fury, and one day he sent me
an urgent message, 'There's a quite unexpected vacancy in a splendid house. Leap at it.'

I was about to leap, rejoicing but alone for my husband was in
Africa, when Orders said 'No. Not that house. Write and ask X's
advice.' This was too much. I had scarcely seen X since he was a
boy, he was now abroad in a senior and onerous diplomatic post
and, although I knew vaguely that his son was at Eton, I did not
consciously know in which house. But Orders would not be si-
lenced, and rather sulkily I wrote. X replied at once that the vacancy had occurred because he had just removed his son from
that house and he did not think it would appeal to us. I doubt
if I could have got the information he gave me from anyone else.

There is a little pendant to this story which almost tempts me
to wonder whether Orders could have been working precognitively
towards a particular goal. I had taken a friend's young son out to
tea and was depositing him at the door of his house when his tutor, Kenneth Wickham, happened to come out. After a few words
Orders said, 'That's your man. Ask him.' Wildly embarrassed—I
had only known the man three minutes—I said quavering, 'Please
will you take my boy next year?'

He looked astounded and said, 'I'm sorry, but I'm afraid I'm
more than full up.'

Then to my horror I heard myself saying, 'I quite understand,
but all the same he has to go to you.'

Luckily he laughed a good deal at this; but when the time came
he did somehow make room for him, and never has any boy been
more fortunate in his tutor.

Kenneth also put up with a good deal. One day he telephoned
to say that the boy was suffering from nausea, fever and other
symptoms suggesting appendicitis, and the doctor advised an immediate operation. Would I agree? I was about to say, 'Yes,' when

Orders said, 'No, he has not got appendicitis. Go to the school and measure his legs.'

Again the conflict. The doctor said an operation was urgent. Orders forbade it. I rushed to the school and against pressure from the doctor and feeling quite crazy went up and did the measuring. One leg was getting on for an inch longer than the other. Knowing the boy's habits I asked, 'Have you been crashing yourself about lately?'

'Well,' he admitted, 'I have found a new way to go downstairs.'

'What is it?'

'You just grip the banisters and fly through the air.'

'I see. And how do you land?'

'On my right foot.'

'Always the same foot?'

'Yes.'

'Ask what he ate yesterday,' said Orders.

'Well, a friend of mine had got some sausages.'

Sausages, high summer and war-time. I liked the idea of that operation less and less. 'Take him to your osteopath in London,' said Orders. We had learnt to trust qualified osteopaths in America, and they had done wonders for us after skiing and other crashes. But I was thoroughly scared at even saying the word osteopath to the very orthodox and highly efficient school doctor. However, to defy Orders was worse, and under the very disapproving eyes of doctor and tutor—'You are taking a *grave* responsibility, Mrs Heywood'—I got an ambulance and carted him off.

His temperature soared sky high, but manipulation corrected a badly twisted back, the test of a specimen indicated that he had eaten mildly contaminated food—and three days later I returned a flourishing child to school. It took rather longer for my jellied knees to return to normal.

In both these cases Orders seemed to stem from an inner knowledge of existing situations. I will now summarize one more of their interventions—it is too long to give in full—because its source is still a puzzle to me. It may even have been precognitive. At least there was plenty of emotional fuel available for it occurred at a moment of acute anxiety.

My husband had scarcely recovered from a long spell of overwork during and after the war when in the late 1940s Fate deprived us of our main source of income. Not long afterwards both our sons came home, and the three decided to cope with this unpleasant situation by designing a small intricate machine for which they believed there might be a market. The project seemed crazy, but they were making headway when an outside strike caused most of their hard-earned orders to be cancelled. At this dire moment Orders drove me out to wander the cold November streets in search of a clue to another line to which the family machine could be adapted. Being very tired and depressed I went resentfully, and was just about to give up at the end of a long, wet, weary afternoon when Orders produced the clue—in a shop window.

I flew home on winged feet, but the family said drearily, 'Sorry, we are just too tired to start big modifications.'

I was acutely disappointed for I 'knew' this was their life line. And it was. Shortly thereafter a request from an outside firm for such a machine gave them the fillip to tackle it, and for years they sold more of that type than of any other.

Usually my Orders come in relation to people with whom I am deeply involved, but such involvement does not seem to be essential. One apparently irrational Order came on behalf of a man I knew but slightly. We did have one link, however: we both felt a passionate interest in E S P.

It was during the Second World War. My husband had been sent to the War Office, and when the journey to and from Sunningdale became too unreliable we took a little house in Westminster. Immediately afterwards he was moved to a distant post where I could not follow him. 'What shall I do with this place?' I asked myself, sitting alone in the empty house. 'Is there any good use to which it could be put?'

'Yes,' said Orders promptly. 'Write at once and ask Mr and Mrs Tyrrell to come and live in it.'

I found this preposterous. Mr Tyrrell was an elderly member of the S.P.R. Council. I had only met him a few times at meetings and had once had supper with him and his wife. Early in the war they had been bombed out of their London flat and had gone to a quiet place in the country where he was now peacefully writing a book.

'It would help the book,' said Orders, 'for him to come to London.' That, I thought, was a tiresome attempt to rationalize an absurd impulse: what elderly man could write better in bomb-ridden London than in the country? However, Orders once more defeated reason, and very apologetically I wrote. The immediate and delighted reply was that my letter had come in the nick of time. The Tyrrells had just been told that their landlord wanted his house back, Mr Tyrrell's book could get no further until he lived near the library of the S.P.R., and he could not afford to set up house again in London.

I owed a lot to those particular Orders. Not only did the Tyrrells spend three years in our house during which Mr Tyrrell's book, *The Personality of Man*, was happily finished, but under the guidance of its author I learnt far more than I should ever have done otherwise about the many problems of tracking down ESP.

I record these incidents to illustrate what I mean by Orders and the conflicts they can create; but they also illustrate other intriguing questions posed by ESP-type experiences. What combination of outward conditions and inner impetus, for instance, enabled those particular impressions to rise to consciousness when others, which might be equally useful, do not? Did the intense concern of a wife and mother for her family cause her to scan—to use an analogy—all the time for information which might be useful to them? And did anxiety provide the emotional fuel which drove the information up to consciousness? But I felt no anxiety or concern about Mr Tyrrell, who was a comparative stranger, when Orders said he ought to come and live in our house; he was, as far as I knew, quite happy and comfortable where he was. Could this, then, have been a reverse situation? Was his ardent desire to get on with his book in London a 'beam'—again I can only use an analogy—which could reach me because we were linked in some inner fashion by our common interest in psychical research? And was I able to bring it up to consciousness because at the right moment I was pondering quietly on what was the best use to make of the house? It is to this kind of question that I will now turn.

CHAPTER XII

The Emergence of ESP

Writing the preceding chapters has brought home to me one thing about myself as experient which hitherto I had not got into focus, partly perhaps because as investigator I have to hold myself rigidly neutral until the existence of a phenomenon has been confirmed beyond question. It is that my own experiences, together with others seen at first hand, have led me to make two assumptions. The first of these is that *even when they do not know it* men and women are reacting all the time to elements in their immediate vicinity which are not perceptible *via* the known senses. (As experiences of this kind can seldom be checked I leave examples until later.) The second assumption is that we are not the encapsulated little entities that Western man believes us to be, but that, as Professor Broad has tentatively postulated, beneath the surface we are in constant telepathic communication with one another, proportionately perhaps to the mental or emotional affinity between particular individuals. Poets have come to similar conclusions. 'No man is an island, intire of itself,' wrote John Donne, 'every man is a peece of the continent, a part of the maine.' And W. B. Yeats held that 'the borders of our minds are ever shifting and that many minds can flow into one another, as it were, and create or reveal a single mind, a single energy'.

Such assumptions may be moonshine, but whether they are or not, for the person who makes them they insistently raise the question: What encourages or inhibits the emergence into consciousness of an extra-sensory signal? Why do some signals rise to the surface while others do not? And why, anyway, do they rise so seldom if they ever rise at all?

One reason for their sporadic appearance may be that very sense of separateness felt by Western man. It is said that in some Oriental and in primitive cultures the consciousness of *I* being separate from *you* is far less strong than in the West, and from these cultures come many travellers' tales of E S P. Again, a whole string of conditions may have to be right at the same moment, and this may only happen very seldom. It is worth remembering, too, that the emergence of other subconscious material, particularly creative ideas, is also sporadic and unpredictable and certainly cannot be commanded to order. Whitehead marvelled at all emergence from deeper levels. 'How miraculous it is,' he said, 'I do not mean thoughts that we have first carefully formulated in our minds and then given words. I mean quite unconscious thoughts which spring instantaneously from the unconscious into words, without any intermediate process being operative that we know of: that is the most amazing thing.' Perhaps the lady who said, 'How can I know what I think till I hear what I've said?' was not being so foolish after all!

Whitehead made another remark which most experients would probably echo. 'I am impressed,' he said, 'by the inadequacy of our conscious thought to express our subconscious. . . . Only at rare moments does that deeper and vaster world come through into conscious thought or expression'.[1]

Professor Beveridge hazards a conjecture as to why intuitive ideas spring full-fledged into consciousness.[2] If, he says, we consciously get at a new idea about a problem in which we are interested by means of step-by-step thinking, we feel pleased and excited. But the subconscious also appears to mull over problems, and *its* pleasure at a new idea may be the fuel which enables that idea to rise to consciousness as an intuition. In any case, he feels sure that an emotion is often associated with an intuition, and he wonders whether scientists who say they never get intuitions are those who also say that they find no joy in new ideas or are deficient in emotional sensitivity.

This line of thought is in harmony with the experient's feeling that emotional fuel can aid the emergence of E S P, and experients would also echo Professor Beveridge's further remarks about intuitive ideas. 'Some,' he says, 'come into consciousness and are grasped . . . some might perhaps fail to appear or only appear fleetingly, and disappear again like the things we were about to say but which slipped away irretrievably before there was a break

[1] As quoted by Lucien Price in *Dialogues of A. N. Whitehead* (Reinhardt, London, 1954).

[2] W. I. B. Beveridge, *The Art of Scientific Investigation* (Heinemann, 1950), p. 72 et seq.

in the conversation.' Again, 'Ideas often make their appearance
on the fringe of consciousness,' and, 'It is a common experience
that new ideas often vanish within a minute or two of their appearance *if an effort is not made to capture them.*' (My italics.)
How like this is to Gilbert Murray's description of his own ESP.
Sometimes the Sceptic will say, 'Well, *I* never experience ESP.
How do you account for that?' Perhaps part of the answer is that
he would never have made an effort to capture a perception on
the fringe of consciousness that he knows he could not have had.

Professor Beveridge speaks yet again for experients when he
says that the factors most adverse to new ideas are interference,
worry and competing interests. 'Messages from the subconscious,'
he adds, 'may not be received at all if the mind is too actively occupied or too fatigued.' The ideal, he suggests, is for it to be
gently ticking over, not actively concerned with the problem involved but not so engrossed in something else that 'it suppresses
anything interesting arising from the subconscious'. Hundreds
of creative thinkers confirm these views. Some say the best time
for new ideas is in the bath. Descartes, Wallace, Poincaré and
Einstein preferred bed.[8] What all this comes to is that to break
through to consciousness spontaneously, creative thought and
ESP seem to like similar conditions; conditions, incidentally,
which obtained in the contemplative lives led by saints and yogis,
to whom tradition so often attributes extra-sensory gifts. Not that
quiet inevitably results in ESP, but at least peaceful surroundings do not force the attention outward in the same disruptive
fashion as jet planes and swarming cars and shrilling telephones
and cocktail parties and rush-hour battles to earn one's daily bread.

As regards breaking through, ESP may be at a disadvantage
compared with a thinker's own ideas about a subject in which he
is already interested. Coming from outside, it may be unfamiliar,
even downright unpleasant. It may also have to evade that biologically useful censor, and, slipping in as it does by the back
door, it certainly has to compete with our natural tendency to

[8] Examples of the emergence of creative ideas will be found in the chapter
on *Genius* in F. W. H. Myers' *Human Personality* (Longman's, 1954), in
Rosamund Harding's *The Anatomy of Inspiration* (Heffer, 1942) and in *The
Creative Process*, edited by Brewster Ghiselin (University of California Press,
1952).

keep our eyes fixed on the outer world through the front door of the senses and to ignore the processes which go on in our own minds. Most people, for instance, seem to have no idea whether they are image or verbal thinkers, or whether they dream in colour or black and white. They could only too easily fail to notice a transient flicker of E S P across a misty corner of the mind.

These difficulties exist within the experient. But in telepathic interaction presumably the agent as well has to be in the right state, and interpersonal conditions must be propitious. Einstein wrote that when a theoretical physicist told him that he was inclined to believe in telepathy, he replied, 'This has probably more relation to physics than to psychology.' The physicist agreed.[4] If so, it is conceivable that the weather—dryness, damp, electrical conditions, even, perhaps, the proportion of positive to negative ions in the air—may take a hand. The extraordinary thing may be, not that E S P is observed so seldom and so sporadically, but that the many conditions needful for its emergence ever combine at all.

To revert to the personal. Clues as to why I pick up one thing and not another are hard to find. To me quiet and a more or less inactive brain are important—and *no expectation* on the part of my conscious mind. Expectation has the added drawback of making it hard for a critical experient not to dismiss a possible extra-sensory impression as inference or 'pure imagination'. Keeping one's balance on the fence is very tricky. Here, for instance, is an experience which I suspect may have been extra-sensory, not only because of the sense of pressure given by Orders, but also because my action was the opposite from what rational expectation would have led me to take. Moreover, the conditions on my side and my husband's fitted neatly into the usual pattern.

One morning in the late forties, very shortly after a stroke of fate had removed our main source of income, I drove my husband to our solicitor's office next door to Sunningdale station, where he had to discuss the resultant sale of our family home. His intention was, after the interview, to catch a train to London which went an hour or so later, but as soon as I left he found that the man he was to meet had been prevented from coming. In conse-

[4] Quoted by A. Vallentin in *Einstein* (Weidenfeld and Nicolson, 1953).

quence he had nothing to do but kick his heels for at least an hour —and there is no better way of causing him to provide emotional fuel than having to kick his heels when very busy at a time of crisis. I, meanwhile, was driving home along a quiet country road which I knew blindfold; my mind, in other words, was mildly occupied but not engrossed. About half a mile away Orders said sharply, 'Go back at once. He wants you,' at which I was not pleased. It made no sense. We had talked over what he would say to the solicitor. I had seen him in at the door, I was busy at home, and the road was twisty, narrow and tiresome to turn in. But Orders insisted, and rebelliously I drove on to a farm gate, turned and went back. When I got to the solicitor's I found a frustrated husband on the doorstep. I was quite popular.

As I have said, I seem more inclined to pick up such minor mishaps to my husband than major crises. (Fortunately, they happen oftener.) I failed, for instance, to get two serious accidents or a narrow shave when he was Military Attaché in Turkey, and a brigand killed the guide in his car with a bullet meant for him. One possible reason for this may be that on such occasions I have happened to be actively engrossed, but another is that when he is on adventure bent I worry—and worry, as Professor Beveridge noted, can inhibit the emergence of subconscious material. So, I suspect, can fear in the experient, or anything else that makes a mental 'buzz'. Another possibility is that on his side my husband may not produce the right kind of emotional fuel in crises, because, provided he can play an active part, he enjoys them thoroughly. What annoy him are minor frustrations, and the repression of his annoyance under a politely impassive exterior may stoke up an extra supply of fuel. Moreover, in many reported cases of crisis telepathy the agent is very frightened; but my husband adores danger and appears to have no fear of death. I always found this hard to believe until I had a chance to check it. He was shaving on the top floor of a house when the noise of a V.1 cut off so near that it seemed to be almost in the room. 'What are we to do?' I asked in the small polite voice of concealed terror.

'There's nothing we can do,' he answered peacefully. I watched him with great care. He did not pause in his shaving, nor did his hand shake.

Unfortunately for me I do not pick up his apparently precognitive flair when he is driving me in a car. This may be partly due to my fear for, at least until old age overtook him, as soon as his hand touched a steering wheel his mood became that of a Paris taxi driver hasting to his loved one in the springtime. I have cowered at his side for forty years on journeys across Europe, Africa and America, and I wish I had noted down how often, in response to a petrified squeak from me, he has said patiently, 'But I knew there was no one round that corner,' or in wild country, 'But I knew that verge—or that bridge—would hold.' (On one occasion in the Balkans he suddenly decided that to one particular bridge he preferred the river bed. That was not a hunch I cared to check.) Equally often he will slow down to a crawl for no reason that is apparent until a child darts out of a hedge or a dog out of a ditch. It is as if in a car his present includes what to me is the immediate future. I once knew his present stretch overnight. A big limousine ran into our small sports car and forced it on to the pavement up against a lamp post.

'It's all right,' he said placidly, 'I dreamt this last night. I know what's wrong. I only have to change the wheel.' He got out, looked, said, 'It's as I thought,' and changed it. There is nothing like a little E S P-type experience to make one wonder about the real nature of what we call time and space.

It has sometimes appeared as if certain items of subconscious knowledge would never have broken through to my conscious self had not an outside event at the right moment triggered them off. Early in 1939 my husband wrote from Egypt that he was about to fly to Salisbury, in Rhodesia, *via* Nairobi, and soon afterwards I read in *The Times* that the engines of a flying boat had failed in a tropical storm off the coast of Portuguese East Africa. The boat had ended up in the sea and the passengers—unnamed— had been dramatically rescued by Africans in canoes. Although on the rational level I knew that my husband was nowhere near the place, I also 'knew' that he was among these passengers. He was. But I doubt if I should have become aware of it consciously had I not read *The Times* that morning.

That impression, if not imaginary, was retrocognitive. It came after the event. Two years later a chance conversation in the right place seems to have triggered off a precognition. At the beginning of May, 1941, I was standing with Gilbert Murray in Parliament

Square, and he said, pointing at the Houses of Parliament, 'Well, they haven't hit them yet!'

I nearly cried out, 'Oh, don't say that,' for as he spoke I 'knew' that they would be hit the following Saturday. But—alas for evidence—I did not say so; he would not care for dramatizing ESP. By the Saturday I also 'knew' that my husband's Club would be hit as well, and when I went to bed was too restless to sleep and read till the early hours of the morning. Then the tension relaxed and I dozed off. Both the House of Commons and the Club got a direct hit that night—the only time during the war. Moreover, it was the only night that my husband decided to leave his bed and go to the ground floor during a raid. He sat by the lift shaft, and the blast from the bomb which hit the bedroom wing blew him along the corridor. On no other night, even after the Normandy landings, was I kept awake by the fear that his sleeping place would be hit, which seems odd in view of my tendency to worry about him; but I worried surprisingly little during the war, perhaps because it transcended personal anxieties. Unfortunately these are not improbabilities that can be assessed statistically.

I happened once at an appropriate moment to open a byeway to the subconscious by means of a ouija board, and I doubt whether the apparent precognition which resulted would have occurred otherwise. I will give the incident in some detail as it illustrates how many questions can be raised by one simple sentence.

A doctor asked me to show him my ouija board working, and we tried it with his finger and mine on the pointer. After it had spelt out some trite remarks I felt a sudden impulse to test what it would write if I could not see the letters. Would that concern the doctor only, or me as well? To make my test I sat down on the floor with my head bent below table level, but my arms stretched up so that two fingers could still rest on the pointer. After a minute or two the doctor said that it had written that George had asked for Frank to be warned to drive with exaggerated care for the next two days. This, he said, meant nothing to him as he had no close links with a George.

What, then, was the origin of that remark, assuming that it was not due to the kind of chance that would eventually bring about the typing of Hamlet by a monkey? George is a common enough name, but it happened to have been that of my husband's much-loved brother, who had been killed not long before. As far as one can guarantee anything, I can guarantee that the doctor, whom I had met only once, had never heard of the brother or of my husband's tendency to spirited driving. But I cannot be sure that I had not casually referred to my husband by his name, Frank.

If I did originate the remark, some part of me must have shown considerable skill in pushing the pointer to the right letters, since my hand was above my head and the board was out of my sight. At the same time this circumstance might have helped to prevent my conscious mind from interfering. Another possibility is that I telepathically transferred a precognition of my own to the doctor's subconscious mind, and it was then able to guide his hand to the letters. If so, why did the message come as from George? I had never had any sense of communication with him or spelt out anything purporting to come from him. In those days too I felt even more convinced that survival of death was unthinkable than I do now. Was the form of the message, then, a way of evading the censor? Or was my subconscious dramatizing to tease me, just because I was so sceptical of survival of death? (In me the level contacted *via* a ouija board has a wry sense of humour.) Or did it seriously think that I might respond more to a warning which appeared to come from a surviving George? Or—I cannot disprove this—did he survive, and had I inadvertently given him a chance to warn his brother?

As I wrote this, two other points occurred to me. The warning might have been due to my husband's own precognitive knowledge which could not emerge in him but could in me. And to word it in that way, implying a knowledge of family affairs which the doctor lacked, might also have been a kind of answer from my subconscious—and I very much wanted one—to the question: Could I influence a ouija board which I could not see?

My courage did not quite run to dismissing the warning as nonsense, but I feared that if I told my husband about it he might laugh and drive even faster. So, feeling a fool as so often before, I said to him, 'Please, just to be kind to me, ask no questions, but for two days drive with exaggerated care.'

The following evening he came in looking really astonished.

'Do you know,' he said, 'if I had not driven with exaggerated care as you asked me to, I should have had no less than three major accidents today.' I could not help being glad that I had had the courage to be a fool.

Finally, here is quite a different type of trigger—the very ordinary name being used by a man I had never heard of. (It was, we learnt later, a false one.) In primitive cultures the use of names is a serious matter; knowledge of a man's name is believed to put one in psychic contact with him. But there are more plausible alternatives for this incident than that very unscientific idea.

The background shows that once more there was plenty of emotional fuel about. It was soon after fate had removed the bulk of our income, and we were both extremely tired. The situation looked far from comfortable to people who, the war apart, had perhaps been too comfortable for too long. Just at that moment a man turned up with an exceptionally clever minor invention, which, like so many inventors, he seemed incapable of marketing properly. Having had experience along that line, my husband thought he might use what at the time I believed to be pretty well all our remaining capital to market it for him and so earn us a modest living. It seemed a good idea and I agreed, and then asked casually, 'What is the man's name?' We both got a shock when he gave it, for a wave of dread and repulsion swept over me so acute that I cried out, 'Oh, don't, don't have anything to do with that man!'

He tried to calm me, but in vain. At last he said, 'But I can't let him down. I've promised.'

At that I cried out desperately, 'Then *give* him the money. Only cut all contact with him.' And I meant it.

Naturally enough my husband thought that stress and fatigue had made me over-emotional, and since the invention was a clever one, he carried on. On the rational level there was no reason why he should not. But he gradually came to suspect that in a subtle fashion the man was making away with our money, and by the time he could confirm this someone else had made a similar discovery and had gone to the police. The man was well-known to them, they arrested him—and while on bail during his trial he hanged himself.

This incident again provokes a string of questions. How could a commonplace name trigger off dread and repulsion so strong that, when very tired and no longer young, I was prepared to sacrifice pretty well all the money I thought we had to get my husband clear of the man? A primitive might say that the name had linked me with him telepathically. But it was an assumed name. Yet there is one hint that I was actually revolted by the man himself, poor creature. One day, after this experience but before my husband had found him out, I happened to pass him in a passage, and although he was very polite I felt I was going to be sick. It was much as I had felt as a child when near the snaky parlourmaid. To me a more likely possibility is that my husband was subconsciously aware that the man was a crook, but was repressing this knowledge on account of his great anxiety to find an additional source of income. So it had to emerge in me. I might also, conceivably, have precognized my husband's distress on hearing that the man had hanged himself. But this is no more than guesswork. Only the study of many similar experiences will provide a clue to the puzzle.

CHAPTER XIII

Agency and Motivation (i)

In the last chapter I tried to illustrate the question: Do factors in the immediate mood or environment of the experient or the agent affect the emergence of a telepathic impression? (The term agent is used here, it will be remembered, simply to denote the person to whose situation the experient reacts.) There are a number of other related questions: Who, for instance, plays the active role, experient or agent? And why? Is telepathy sometimes or always a combined operation? Can any long-term psychological motive for it ever be discerned? And so on. I will try to illustrate one or two such questions.

It is hard to know what jumping-off place to choose when considering a process about which so little is known, but as emotion of some kind so often seems to accompany an observed telepathic situation, it may be as good a one as any. At least the experient can throw some light on what his own surface emotions on particular occasions appeared to be.

But first, what have investigators to say about telepathy from the outside? The pioneers of psychical research and most of their successors took for granted that the agent was the active partner; he projected his thought or feeling on to the experient. Some, however, have suggested a different picture, that the relation between the two may create a psychic field, in which, on the analogy of two bits of iron in a magnetic field, they are both contained. But Professor Sir Cyril Burt, although he is one of those who envisage the possibility of psychic fields, has pointed out that the idea is merely a model, to facilitate thinking.

In the early 1950s Dr Louisa Rhine put forward a view which was the opposite of that usually held. It was that in telepathy the experient, not the agent, is generally if not always the active partner. She had been driven to this unexpected conclusion by the long-term study of the many thousand spontaneous E S P-type experiences which had been sent in to the Parapsychology Laboratory at Duke University.[1] (As I said earlier, two somewhat less scientific authorities, the purported discarnate communicators of Mrs Leonard and Mrs Willett both complained that their sensitives were liable to take over the active role and rummage in their minds for material which they, the communicators, did not want transmitted.) Once the idea of the experient as the active partner has been suggested, it is not hard to imagine that a person who is emotionally drawn to another might all the time be 'scanning'— to use the best available analogy—for him or her subconsciously, and that every now and then the right combination of circumstances, including, perhaps, fuel in the shape of a spurt of emotion in the agent, might enable a particular item to break through to consciousness. My impulses to take my husband a torch in the black-out and to return to him at the solicitor's office, when on the rational level I felt sure he did not need me, may be examples of such a combination of circumstances.

Observations by some psychoanalysts also conform to this pattern. They say that items in their patients' dreams occasionally correspond to events in the analysts' own lives about which the dreamers could not have known. Höllos, a Hungarian psychoanalyst, reports having observed many cases of apparent telepathy in his own work.[2] Perhaps during the period of transference the patient will 'scan' for an analyst whose life he temporarily longs to share. In the early 1950s, with somewhat embarrassed amusement a young analyst gave me an example of such apparent telepathy. Shortly before his marriage he went to bed with his future wife for the first time, and for the great occasion she wore an extremely striking and unusual garment. A day or two later a patient reported a dream of just such a garment. But he did not connect this with the analyst.[3] One may guess that analysts do not always feel in a position to report such cases because, if these

[1] For researchers Dr Rhine has analysed the result of her survey of spontaneous E S P-type experiences in a series of articles in the *Journal of Parapsychology* from 1951 onwards. For the general public she has also given an account of her work in *Hidden Channels of the Mind* (Gollancz, 1961).

[2] See *Psychoanalysis and the Occult*, edited by George Devereux (International Universities Press, New York, 1953). Also Jan Ehrenwald, *Telepathy and Medical Psychology* (Allen and Unwin, 1947) and *New Dimensions of Deep Analysis* (Allen and Unwin, 1954).

[3] Jung records in his *Memoirs* a roughly parallel case in which the doctor,

speculations are on the right lines, the cases would be liable to relate to emotional situations in the analysts' own lives, and even for the rest of us to make public certain incidents could endanger a friendship. Long ago, for instance, I tried to help a left-wing artist who thought it positively immoral even to be clean, much less well-dressed. One night I dreamt that I saw her wearing long white kid gloves, and three weeks later I was amused to meet her at a Chelsea-type party, wearing a take-off of formal evening dress and just such gloves. Had my subconscious, I wondered, precognized this incident to give me a clue to her character? I asked a psychiatrist friend what he thought it could mean.

'Could you have suspected her of a little hypocrisy?' he said laughing. Of course! I had been averting my eyes from that knowledge for some time.

The autobiographies of certain well-known spiritualist mediums suggest that childhood experiences may have been a permanent stimulus to their E S P, which, whether or not they were, as they believed, in touch with extra-mundane sources of information, seems on occasion to have been real enough. The E S P of Mrs Osborn Leonard, for instance, looks like a natural antidote to an appalling introduction to death which she suffered at the age of eight. Another medium has said that he felt his to be compensation for his acute feelings of inferiority in youth; it was wonderful to have people hanging on his words instead of laughing at him. In such cases of special ability the experient may always play the active role, but in ordinary devoted families, such as my own, one can envisage the possibility of mutual 'scanning' and also of subconscious appeals by one member to the other for support in difficult circumstances. These two factors together might create

---

Jung, experienced sensations which corresponded with a patient's situation. Jung had pulled a patient out of a psychogenic depression, but he feared that the jealous attitude of the patient's wife might cause the depression to recur and warned him to communicate at once should it show signs of doing so. Unfortunately, the man lacked the courage to communicate in face of his wife's hostility, and so Jung heard nothing. One night Jung was awakened by the conviction that someone had come into the room, and also by a dull pain, as if something had struck his forehead and then the back of his skull. He learnt the next day that during the night the patient had shot himself in the forehead, and the bullet had lodged in the back wall of the skull. Jung writes that he knows many other cases in which the relationship between doctor and patient led to parapsychological phenomena.

conditions in which subconscious telepathic interaction was continuous; but whether or not it broke through to consciousness would probably depend on how engrossed, agitated or active the experient was at the time.

It only occurred to me recently that a whole series of similar ESP-type impressions might in themselves suggest a motive for them in the experient when an isolated impression would not; and if a plausible motive were found, that in its turn would support the conjecture that the experient had played the active role. A plausible motive for ESP in my family is concern for each other's welfare, for we are very closely linked, and in 1960 one of the few investigators known to me who is also an experient, told me of some personal experiences which seem to suggest a long-term motive in her. She had had a series of visual images of unusual objects which at the time seemed quite pointless. Nevertheless, she felt that they were precognitive, and in her role of investigator she at once made a drawing of each one and had it dated and counter-signed by a responsible person. In every case, she said—though perhaps many months later—she came unexpectedly on an object in the outer world which closely resembled her image. 'So many coincidences can hardly have come about by chance,' I thought, 'I must watch for a motive.'

She soon supplied one which seemed to me very plausible. One day, she said, she 'saw' and drew a curious square coloured rose design, and later on she and her husband came on just such a design on a tile in the Cairo Museum, a place she had never visited before. 'At that,' she went on, her face lighting up, 'my husband said that at last he had to admit that ESP must be a fact.'

'Did that please you?' I asked.

'Oh, yes, indeed it did,' she said, and her voice revealed how much she had longed for him to recognize the reality of her ESP. I understood this longing well enough. One has a curious sense of isolation when even a stranger rejects as nonsense an impression which one feels, but cannot prove, to be extra-sensory. It is as if music one heard in the distance were to be dismissed with contempt as only the wind in the trees. How much stronger would be that feeling in a devoted wife whose husband doubted the existence of something she had experienced and studied for much of her life; strong enough, perhaps, to provide the emotional fuel which enabled the precognitions by which at last he was converted to break through.

What brought this line of thought to a head was my attempt to find some point in a series of over twenty E S P-type impressions which I had had in connection with a French-Canadian friend, Paul, during and shortly after the Second World War. I noted down nineteen of them, though not very methodically, and seldom, which was a pity, in advance of confirmation. There were two reasons for this. I had recently joined the S.P.R. and had discovered that spontaneous E S P-type experiences, however carefully documented, were quite out of fashion as evidence of its existence. So there really seemed no point, when overworked, of driving oneself to such strictness if it served no purpose. Moreover, until the more trivial impressions were confirmed I did not always realize that they might be due to E S P. Professor Broad has pointed out that this may often happen. Experients do not necessarily recognize E S P for what it is.

Some of my impressions about Paul were useful. They warned me that he would not be able to keep an appointment with me or a member of my family, or that he had suddenly been taken ill. But others seemed pointless. Now, on re-reading them, I asked myself, as an analyst asks of a dream: Why did I have them? Was there any long-term motive behind the series?

As I studied them, two such motives appeared possible. To make these clear I have to sketch the background.

During the war I shared my mother's house at Sunningdale, and although she was the kindest of parents my odd ways often bewildered her. This made me tend towards caution when we talked together. My husband was away and the work which fell to the lot of middle-aged women with children was not dramatic. Mine was to run the local W.V.S., to chase the village women to mend and knit for the Forces, the children to pick rosehips, and the old men to dig for victory. I was responsible for the local emergency food supplies, and at home there were vegetables and fruits to be grown and bottled. There were also evacuees. Most of the help they needed seemed to be along such unromantic lines as curing their progeny of worms in crude Mediterranean fashion with garlic.

I recite this boring list of humdrum activities just because it was so boring, and I think that the need to vary it could have driven me to E S P in relation to Paul, because he provided the only colourful antidote available, most of my friends being away at the war. I met him like this. As a Governor of the English Speaking Union I went to London for a night or two most weeks, to help organize private hospitality for overseas troops and do other odd jobs. While there, said my husband, I had better do something about a Canadian who had served under him in France. This was Paul. After a serious wound he was now marooned in the War Office and rebelling, as temperamental men of letters always do, against routine. Being gay and witty, he made me laugh, and we got into the habit of stoking up at intervals during a quick lunch with frivolous escapist talk about music, the theatre and books, mostly the books he one day hoped to write. Writing was a celestial sport I had never dared to aspire to, and listening to writers talking about their work was the next best thing. It seems plausible then that the desire to continue these gay, inspiriting and instructive conversations provided the emotional fuel for my E S P-type flashes, for they were inclined to be about work he was mulling over in his mind. One day, for instance, I felt so strongly that I had to say the word 'They' to him, that, absurd as it seemed, I noted it in my diary. When I did so he replied, laughing, that he had thought of using the word as a title for his next book.

On another occasion he exclaimed, interrupting me, 'You can't say that. You've already said it in my book.' The Prince Rupert-Cromwell impression I mentioned earlier was connected with him and so was the impulse which I resisted to telephone and make him laugh. Yet another time, when sitting quietly with my husband, who was on leave, I remarked out of the blue, 'I know how to write a biography . . .' and then described a curious oblique method of studying the effect of a man's personality on other people and writing from that. I had never had such an idea before. Indeed I had never considered the technique of writing biographies: if I had I should not have expected it to interest my husband; nor did I think that biography was at all in Paul's line. However, when next we met he said that he had been toying with the idea of writing the biography of a certain statesman in just the fashion I had suggested.

It may be here that our minds were working parallel, though, knowing our minds, I think it most unlikely. But parallel thinking does not explain the occasions when I 'knew'—and rang up to confirm—that Paul had suddenly been taken ill. (On one of them he had been whisked away for an emergency operation.) Possibly my nursing instinct, which his many ailments had certainly aroused, can account for these.

As I said, when such impressions warned me that he would be prevented from keeping appointments, they served a practical purpose. One of these warnings seemed to be followed by a tip from my subconscious to check that it had indeed been extra-sensory. After breakfast one morning I sat down for a moment's quiet before tackling the day's work, and when I did so the thought flashed into my mind that it was no good visiting Paul in hospital that afternoon as I had planned to do. I rang up to check this. 'He's in the bath,' said the nurse, 'but I know he's been told to go for an X-ray this afternoon. Could you come tomorrow?'

'He might have let me know,' I thought, mildly aggrieved. Then came another flash. 'When you see him tomorrow you must say, "Thank you for your telepathic message." I assumed this to be ironical, but as my lips kept forming the words in the bus next day I did say it, though still believing on the conscious level that I was doing so as a bit of frivolity because Paul was inclined to jeer at the idea of E S P. To my surprise he answered quite seriously, 'Yes, I thought I'd check that telepathy of yours. Just as I was about to have my bath I heard that I had to go for an X-ray this afternoon. So I sent you a mental message to ring me up. If you didn't I was going to ring you.'

That was all very nice, but it had one drawback. Hitherto Paul had merely laughed at E S P, but now he seemed to recoil from it. He said it invaded his privacy, ignoring my rather sour comment that, on the contrary, he seemed to be invading mine. Thereafter it was less easy to check impressions which might have been telepathic.

I will finish with two trivial incidents which one is almost forced to dismiss as chance coincidences until study of the psychological background makes them plausible as examples of E S P. After years of rationing, food in general had got on my nerves, for there was a constant conflict between my very undomestic nature and a kind of obsession that, whatever the difficulty, it was up to me somehow to provide plenty of succulent nourishment for my husband, two enormous sons and the stray friends they would bring home, 'for a good meal, Mummy, please.'

Among our strays was Paul, and he, owing to his various ailments and French blood, was harder than the others to cope with about food. In consequence I felt specially inadequate when he came. One day I had a sudden impulse, to which nothing seemed to lead up, to ask him if he liked peaches in champagne, though why I should think of that exotic beverage out of the blue I could not imagine; I certainly had none to give him and had not tasted it myself since a luncheon party at the French Summer Embassy on the Bosphorus in the long forgotten world of 1929. But Paul beat me to it. When he came in a day or two later he said, 'You'll never guess what I've been having—peaches in champagne!'

Soon after that I dreamt that I had offered him whitebait for dinner. I dislike whitebait and never cook it. When we next saw him he said he had got hold of some tinned whitebait, which I did not know existed. A third such impression had a practical purpose. I felt that he was inadvertently burning a wine ration card of ours and telephoned hastily to try to save it—but too late.

These trivial impressions illustrate another point made by Professor Broad about telepathy in general, that such incidents could easily have gone unnoticed had not Paul happened to come in and to take enough interest in food to mention his unexpected treats.

With the end of the war came release from my more humdrum activities, and the mental stimuli which had for a time been provided by Paul alone again became available elsewhere. Also his health improved. Concurrently, my impressions about him faded out, and when he accepted a post in an American university, they ceased altogether.

I do not want to suggest that in telepathic interaction the experient must always be the active partner. I doubt if that was so when I invited Mr Tyrrell to live in our house, or on the occasions when I have communicated with someone towards whom I felt pretty neutral, to find that they were needing to talk to me. This sort of thing can practically never be evidential, but on occasion experients may know themselves to be acting against their conscious inclination. In the nineteen fifties, for instance, I felt an urge to telephone a woman who had an invalid mother and whom I knew moderately well, to ask if a small loan would be any use to her. This was embarrassing. We were not on money-lending terms, she was proud and highly strung, and I gave in to the pressure reluctantly, fearing that she might feel insulted. But she said, 'Good gracious, I was just wondering where on earth I could find the money to get mother the special diet she has been ordered.' I knew they were not well off, but had no idea that things were as bad as that.

Even here there was some link; I knew and quite liked the woman. But the occasional case where there is no such link is very puzzling. One day, for instance, I saw my younger son look up the name of a street in the map of London because, so he told me later, he had 'known' that when he went out someone was going to ask him where it was and he did not know. This happened as he had foreseen within an hour. Chance? Perhaps. Yet he has never looked up a street for that reason and not been asked for it. But if it was not chance, what was the link between two total strangers? What kind of mental broadcasting may be implied?

CHAPTER XIV

Agency and Motivation (ii)

Even people who are prepared in principle to envisage E S P differ a good deal in their reactions to the various forms it can take. Some will accept telepathy, but jib at precognition. Others swallow any mental phenomenon, but reject the idea that mind could ever directly affect matter apart from the body with which it is immediately associated. Others, again, can envisage anything, however unlikely, provided that it is confined to what they call 'this world', but the suggestion that something in man may survive the death of the body either shocks them—or, nowadays, merely bores them. One clever man said to me that he did not see how anyone could be the least degree interested in such an idea.

These reactions seem to be deeply ingrained. Take my own case. I accept E S P readily enough, having, as I have come to believe, experienced it on a small scale all my life. But some inner quirk—or is it conditioning by current orthodoxy?—makes me jib at the idea of being able to affect matter at a distance by mental means, and far more at the suggestion of any form of survival after death, even when I myself have experienced what looks like first hand evidence of it. The writing of this chapter, for instance, was put off for months, simply because in it I have to confess to the experience of meeting people who had recently died. That kind of experience causes the sceptic and experient in me to become locked in a battle which neither seems able to win, and as a result I cannot make up my mind whether incidents such as the following were due to contact with something other than myself, or to 'pure imagination', or what will you. But I am pretty sure that it would be dishonest to funk reporting them because of my own scepticism or because they will doubtless cause some people to label me an ardent Believer like Mr Black.

I sometimes try to escape from this quandary by seeking for psychological reasons why these apparent contacts with the dead, though unexpected, may still have been self-induced. One reason could be my childhood picture of death. In those days my ultimate destination seemed clear enough: black devils and scarlet flames awaited the wicked; I was wicked; so there you were. But hell seemed a long way off, and I remember my childish reaction to the interminable drone of the Litany as one of boredom, not of gloom. I might be a sinner but I was not a miserable one. And they did say God was kind. Then in adolescence came the Haeckel bombshell: matter was all in all and the joints of the Universe creaked. Beauty, love, God, the life of the spirit, were all moonshine. So too presumably were the flames of hell, but the process of dying still seemed frightening and I still half hoped to survive it, moonshine or no. And I also felt that no effort was too great to save a fellow being from death.

Sometimes before going to sleep I ask my subconscious to comment on this or that in a dream, and very occasionally it deigns to do so, perhaps by giving me a symbolic tip. Once when I could not see my way ahead it produced a dream of myself as a little black crow which was frantically trying to escape by running in a hysterical fashion from side to side of a step on a high staircase. All I could see was the wooden face of the next step. Then Something said, 'Jump!' I jumped obediently on to the next step—and the view from there was quite different. 'You could have done that before,' said the Something.

Not long ago, in the hope of getting at some hidden urge or fear which might explain my extra-mundane experiences—or my rejection of them—I asked my subconscious for its views on survival after death. But it vouchsafed no dream. Next morning, however, I found myself whistling an old-fashioned tune which for the moment I could not locate. 'Why whistle that?' I wondered, and then its words slipped into my mind: 'John Brown's body lies a-moulderin' in the grave. . . . But his soul goes marching on.'

What on earth put that tune into my head? Then I remembered my question of the night before. Was this merely a laggard associated idea? Or an oblique intimation that subconsciously I did accept the possibility of survival? Or merely that I wanted to? In that case, said the sceptic in me gleefully, my subconscious might have cooked up my apparent meetings with the dead to bring my recalcitrant reason into line.

To illustrate this type of experience I shall give the two apparently extra-mundane contacts which made the deepest and most lasting impression on me, and in which I felt vividly aware of being urgently approached by a friend. Without prejudice to what really caused them I shall write as if my impressions were correct, partly for clarity, but partly too because this is a record of experiences and in neither case *at the time* did I doubt that the person I had known in life was present.

The background to the first was Washington in the thirties. The diplomatic merry-go-round whirled madly enough to dim the threat of war in distant Europe, and I whirled with it, for when my husband joined the Foreign Service I packed my inner life away in mothball, foolishly assuming that my sole job now was to make friendly contact wherever we went. Not that this was unenjoyable: the world seemed full of friendly people, and it was only too easy to dance like a mayfly in the sun and ignore the fact that such a life was little more than a masked ritual, practically devoid of real communication.

At parties we often met a beautiful and seductive woman called Julia, who was also kind hearted in the nicest American way. We both felt drawn to her for she made us laugh, but a soap bubble would have counter-weighed any talk we had together. One hot summer's day Julia and I were idling with some friends round the swimming pool of a millionaire. No one appeared to have a thought in the world beyond enjoying the sun which dappled our mahogany bodies through the trees. Suddenly she thrust out her hands. 'Read them for me,' she said. (What happened when as a joke I embarked on hand-reading I will tell in Chapter XVI.) Laughing, I took her hands and looked at them, and then heard myself saying, very gravely, 'You will never find what you are looking for in this world, will you?'

She replied, equally gravely, 'No.'

This startled me. It is always a shock when another order of things erupts, like Poseidon, from a foaming sunlit sea; but this time, as usual, the foam swept over it as our care-free friends surrounded us, and the moment of truth was gone. A few weeks later Julia gave a farewell cocktail party before flying to Peru on a visit, and at it she brought me a snapshot of herself, saying, 'This is for you, Rosalind.'

I made a futile cocktail-party reply, 'Oh, surely you mean for Frank?' (my husband) but she said seriously, 'No, I mean for you.' At that Orders said, 'Take it. This is important;' and so I thanked her quietly and took the snapshot.

A day or two later the news arrived that her plane had crashed in the Andes with no survivors. Then followed a strange forty-eight hours, which, whether or not they were self-induced, have at least enabled me to sympathize with people who feel themselves to be mediums or even possessed. I could not get Julia out of my head—not the crash, not any sense of disaster, just her. Even when driving my car I found myself muttering her name, 'Julia, Julia, Julia!'

This puzzled me. It was not natural. Of course, the news of her death was a shock, as it always is when someone very much alive suddenly ceases to exist. But much as we liked her, she had in no way been part of our lives, and my constant thought of her did not make sense. I supposed, however, that the suddenness of her death had been more of a shock than I had realized.

Two days later, most unusually, I found myself with a free afternoon; no parties, the servants out, a glorious pause. 'I'll just write my condolences to Julia's mother,' I thought, 'and then I'll lie down on the garden room sofa and do nothing, nothing at all.'

The letter was a feeble effort, shy, stiff and conventional. I felt ashamed of it, but could do no better for I hardly knew Julia's mother, I had little in common with her, and I did not believe that anything of Julia had survived the destruction of her body. When finished I put it down on my desk with a sigh of relief and then settled myself on the sofa beside it to enjoy the lovely peace. I did not enjoy it long. Although our house stood back from the road in a little-used sidestreet and its garden side was utterly quiet, a few minutes later a Viennese woodcut which was hanging at the far side of the desk fell with a sudden crash to the ground. Very puzzled, I ran over and picked it up. It was undamaged and the cord intact. I looked at the nail. It was just as it should be. Then why and how had the woodcut fallen? I was standing by my desk trying to puzzle out this conundrum when my eye caught the letter to Julia's mother, and at that inside my head I heard Julia speak. She spoke in no uncertain terms. 'Don't send that silly letter,' she said. 'Go to my mother now, straight away, and tell her to stop all that ridiculous mourning at once. I'm very happy and I can't stand it.'

This sudden eruption of the remote 'other' caught me quite unawares, but at the moment I had no more doubt that it was Julia conveying to me her urgent wishes than I doubt it when my husband asks me to pass him the honey at breakfast. But I also had no doubt that were I to rush off to Julia's mother with this extraordinary story, my husband being at the British Embassy the town would buzz with talk. The more I hesitated the more insistent 'Julia' became, until at last I rang my husband and said, 'I don't know what to do.' As usual he settled the thing at once. 'Better be a fool than a knave,' he said. 'Go, if you feel you ought to.'

At that, feeling indeed every kind of fool, I got out my car and went. What made the situation yet more embarrassing was that at the time I knew nothing of the conventions of Americans from the Southern States in face of death, and ignorantly assumed that Julia's mother would behave like mine in similar circumstances, wear her ordinary clothes and hide her grief under a mask of frozen normality. If this were so, to barge in and ask her to stop an excessive display of mourning seemed both pointless and rude. However, on arrival at her house I found all the blinds down and in the hall a covey of melancholy women, talking in whispers and looking like crows. 'May I see Mrs Howard?' I asked them.

They looked shocked. 'Certainly not,' they said, 'she's in bed, mourning.'

That settled it. 'I must see her,' I insisted, and after much protest they took me up to her room. There, indeed, was the poor woman, alone, in the dark, in bed. Intensely embarrassed, for I supposed this was by her own choice, I got out my message, expecting to be thrown out at once as mad or impertinent. But her face lit up. 'I knew it,' she cried, 'I knew she'd hate it, and I didn't want it. I shall get up and stop it at once!'

On me the effect of her response was curious. From that moment all sense of Julia's presence vanished: it was as if, content, she had gone off at once on her own affairs, and from then on I thought of her no more than was normal, and certainly with no sorrow. I was told later that the wife of the Counsellor in another Embassy had also given the mother a similar message from

Julia, whom, she said, she had seen. I did not go into this. I was not yet a member of the S.P.R. and I wanted the story to die down quickly.

That incident again illustrates the inevitable difference of attitude between experient and investigator, seeking for evidence. At the time, as experient, I felt no doubt that some inner part of Julia had known of her approaching death and was happy about it, and that the hand-reading incident and gift of her photograph were both part, so to speak, of a *Gestalt*, out of time as we know it, which somehow helped her to make the necessary contact with me after death. To any investigator such an idea would be mere fantasy. The most he could admit would be that I had taken action which embarrassed me for reasons which did not fit the facts as I knew them, and that my action had turned out to be relevant. He could, if he accepted telepathy, attribute this to telepathic contact between Julia's mother and myself. The part of me which cannot envisage survival jumps at this explanation, but as experient I cannot feel that it takes account of all the facts. As far as I can tell, I do not experience telepathy to that extent with people with whom I feel so little linkage, nor can I quite discount my awareness of Julia's personality and of her passionate desire that the ostentatious mourning should cease at once. So I am left, as usual, on the fence.

From an investigator's point of view there is no evidence that my second apparent meeting with a discarnate friend was due to anything but my own subconscious wishful thinking. The meeting was entirely unexpected, and the friend was Vivian Usborne, the naval inventor, who had been kind to me as a youthful V.A.D. in Macedonia, and who was the first person to share my 'obstinate questionings of sense and outward things'. Since my marriage our lives had scarcely overlapped until in the early 1950's, nearly thirty years later, we found ourselves living within a stone's throw of each other in London. Then we picked up easily where we had left off; but it was not to be for long as Vivian was soon smitten by a lingering but incurable disease. By now he had come to feel, like me, that at death man snuffed out like a candle, and he lamented bitterly that all the many ideas still simmering in his head would never come to fruition. I had in honesty to agree with him.

At his funeral I felt nothing but profound relief at his escape from frustration and suffering—and selfish relief, too, that I no longer had to witness it; I had no sense of his presence at all. About ten days later I went early one morning to get a painting by him which had been given to me. It is perhaps relevant that I was hastening to another appointment in which I was emotionally involved and felt no nostalgic longing for Vivian. As I hurried into his room to fetch the picture I was shocked by a sickening blast of what I have come to call the smell of death. I am never quite sure whether this is physical or what a sensitive might call borderline—though he would be hard put to it to tell an investigator what he meant by that. Then, in staggering contrast (at the time it seemed almost deliberate, but that idea should probably be written off as imagination), I ran slap into 'Vivian' himself, most joyfully and most vividly alive. I pulled up sharply as one would on running into a friend in the street, and then came an experience which it is extremely hard to describe without sounding either flat and meaningless or over-dramatic. As with 'Julia', I felt 'Vivian' communicate inside my mind, and I shut my eyes and stood very still to attend better. He conveyed in some fashion so intimate that the best word seems to be communion, pretentious though that sounds, that he had been entirely mistaken in expecting extinction at death. On the contrary, he now had scope, freedom and opportunity beyond his wildest dreams. The emphasis was not merely on being alive but on this magnificent expansion of opportunity. Then I too seemed to be caught up into the quality of his situation—but not into its form. I experienced no forms and no images.

For a few moments I stood very still, acutely aware of the striking contrast between the smell of death and 'Vivian's' intensity of life—it was as if they were in a different order of things—and then I remembered my duty and 'said' to him, 'This is wonderful, but you've given me no evidence. What can I say to the S.P.R.?'

(I hope that my attempt to describe the immediacy of the purported Julia's communication with me will have made it clear that 'said' is far too remote a word to use for this intimate kind of united awareness. It feels, as Gilbert Murray said of his own telepathic experience, like a kind of co-sensitivity.)

'Vivian's' response to my question was emphatic and immediate. 'I cannot give you evidence. You have no concepts for these conditions. I can only give you poetic images.'

At that, far, far above me, I saw—with the inner eye—an immense pair of white wings flying in a limitless blue sky. Though at first an image of such Victorian obviousness seems absurd, it was in fact an entirely apt expression of the scope, opportunity and freedom into which for a few moments I felt caught up. But it was only for a few moments. I quickly became aware that I could not hold the absorbed state which contact with 'Vivian' demanded, and very soon had to say reluctantly, 'Good-bye, I must drop now.'

Then I dropped—down to the empty room and the smell of death.

I hope it is clear that at the time this experience seemed completely normal and the invisible 'Vivian' as real as a friend one meets in the street. I felt nothing but delight at learning how magnificently happy he was and how wide the scope he now had for his brilliant inventive mind. This lack of fear is common to many experients.

I have had several other experiences connected with the recently dead, but though impressive to me at the time, they were more fleeting and less detailed than the two I have quoted, and to record them would be monotonous. They all had one of two things in common, either a sense of contemporary purpose on the part of the dead, or an urge to action on my part, and in this they differed from my experience of the phenomenon known as haunting, in which, whatever causes it, the sense of urgency is usually lacking. One point is perhaps worth noting. Only on two occasions did I feel that the discarnate person had any spatial relation to myself. In a vague way Julia seemed to be in front of me, somewhat to the right, and when, shortly after the death of the late Lady Rhondda, I seemed to feel her very purposeful presence, she was almost behind me, out to the left. But on that occasion her concern was not with me but with her friend and executrix, Theodora Bosanquet.

I cannot be sure of the cause of my experiences, but I can be sure that they occurred. They could be more easily swept aside as pure imagination were they unique. But they are not. Thousands far more impressive have been reported throughout the ages and from every culture, and it is probably a safe bet that yet more are not mentioned for fear of what 'people would say'. Many, too, have been carefully checked by such bodies as the S.P.R. and the American S.P.R., whereas mine rest on nothing but my own word. Even so, they may at least demonstrate the conflict which can be created when experience contradicts the official beliefs of the society in which one lives.

CHAPTER XV

Dreams

Dreams are a well known route for slipping past the censor, and in the past it was taken for granted that they could have an extra-sensory and even precognitive content. The wives of both Caesar and Pilate, for instance, are said to have had warning dreams before their husbands were involved in disaster.

But even when dreams appear to be precognitive, and the dreamer could not have obtained his information by sensory means, investigators are still inclined to look on them with a chilly eye, on the very reasonable ground that so many people dream so often that some dreams must coincide with reality merely by chance. And the investigator can never feel at first hand the emotional effect of a dream about a forthcoming crisis, or one repeated over the years which is ultimately fulfilled. It is an interesting point that some potentially disastrous events are said to have been modified owing to a previous dream.[1]

Unfortunately I can contribute no such impressive material. I have frequent and vivid dreams of which some contain obvious warnings about my own folly and others constructive advice in symbolic form. I remember only four which show even flickers of possible E S P, and they could scarcely be more trivial. For three of the four plausible motives were evident—two were the dreams already recorded of whitebait and long white gloves—but in the fourth I have as yet been able to see no point at all.

Psychologists may find some reason for my shortage of dream as opposed to waking material, but I cannot guess what it is. It does not stem from discouragement in youth, for the case of apparent E S P about which my mother spoke most freely, and indeed proudly, was an apparently precognitive dream of her youth. In this a man went mad in church and came dashing down

[1] For examples of precognitive dreams see *Proceedings* and *Journal* of S.P.R. and American S.P.R., J. W. Dunne, *An Experiment with Time* (Faber, 1934) and *Intrusions* (Faber, 1955), and Louisa Rhine, *Hidden Channels of the Mind* (Gollancz, 1962).

the aisle towards her. It gave her such a shock that she told both her maid and her sister early the next morning—a Sunday—and when she did go to Church later on in the day, the unnerving and unusual event took place as in her dream.

My husband and younger son have both had dreams which corresponded with subsequent events and as a child my son seemed to take them as quite normal. I discovered this when he was nine years old. He and his brother came out from school in England to spend their summer holidays with us at Rehoboth, a seaside village in Delaware. On arrival he said casually, 'I know this place. I've dreamt it. I know what's there and there [pointing east and south] but not what's there and there [pointing west and north].' I replied equally casually, for I never discussed E S P with the children, 'Well, if you do, lead us down to the sea.'

The way to the sea was obvious enough, one walked downhill, but what was less obvious was our flowered sun umbrella, which was one of hundreds on an enormous beach. Without hesitation he threaded his way between them until he reached it. I followed. 'How did you know that one was ours?' I asked.

'I dreamt the pattern on it.' The pattern was very distinctive and like no other on the beach.

'Do you often dream ahead?'

'Oh, yes, it's very useful at school.' He again said this as indifferently as he would have said that it was useful to be able to swim if you fell out of a boat.

Chance apart, on the face of it this dream seems to have been precognitive, but it might have been due to telepathic interaction with me—we were very close—for I had already explored the parts of Rehoboth he seemed to know. On the other hand they were the parts he himself frequented later on. Chance? Precognition? Telepathy? As so often, the detective must reserve judgment.

To revert to my own dreams. The next, though absurdly trivial, again provides some problems in psychological detection. With whom did it originate, my husband or me? And why? We practically never mention our dreams to each other, but just before the war one of mine was so out of character that I thought it might amuse him. It was that he had taken me to a lush *haute couture* establishment and bought me a gorgeous trailing blue evening dress. 'Why,' he said, 'I dreamt that too,' and we laughed together, for he would have gone to Purgatory rather than to a dressmaker, and it would never have occurred to me to squander the family funds on unnecessarily exotic garments, even in the days when my clothes were still part of the tools of our trade. All the same I was an ordinary woman and a bit of a perfectionist and when he was a diplomat I had sometimes hankered after 'the very very best' in clothes. Perhaps this repressed desire was stronger than I realized, and now that he had left the service, war was looming, and clothes seemed of less than no importance, it may have seeped through the censorship and provided enough emotional fuel to cause him to dream my dream too. For he would always try to get me the moon if I let him know I wanted it.

The next dream interests me because I can see no motive for it; also it appeared to be linked with my husband's subsequent behaviour. If that link was not a chance coincidence, was the dream precognitive or telepathic? Anyway it must have some latent content. Why did I dream it? What was it trying to tell me?

The dream was in vivid colour. I was walking along a track across a flat field towards a farm, and beside me was a tall man leading a little brown pear-shaped sharp-nosed animal by a string which was tied round its middle. I knew he was going to exterminate it and I was sad, but I told myself not to be sentimental as one species could not be allowed to overbreed to the detriment of others. My husband is usually preoccupied and in a hurry at breakfast and seldom draws my attention to anything in the paper, apart from an occasional cartoon or new type of car. But next morning he said, 'Look at this,' and showed me two pictures on the back page of the *Guardian*. One was of a Norfolk farmer holding a dead South American coypu by the tail and the other was of a heap of coypu which had been shot in an effort to exterminate them. A pair had escaped from a private owner and they were breeding rapidly and becoming a pest. I exclaimed, 'Oh, it's my little animal,' for the resemblance was exact, except that my coypu had some small lighter spots on its back. As I said, it was not in character for my husband to show me those photographs. Was he then subconsciously aware of my dream?

I sometimes try out such incidents on psychical researchers to watch their instinctive reactions. I tried this one on a friend who came to dine next day, half hoping that he would enjoy with me a little psychological detection as to why I had had the dream. But the fear to which psychical researchers have so forcibly been conditioned, of envisaging even the remote possibility that E S P could have come into such a minor incident, showed at once. Without asking me how clearly I had seen the animal, he said, very kindly, 'You see, Rosalind, there have been some photos of badgers in the papers lately. Badgers also have long snouts and those photos were doubtless the origin of your dream.'

It did not seem any use pointing out that the dream animal was only about three feet away and that its dark pointed ratlike nose was as like the black and white snout of a badger as a donkey is like a zebra.

Postscript

Typing a fair copy of this chapter stirred the sceptic in me to protest that to take such utterly trivial dreams seriously really did not make sense. How far more likely they were to be due to chance. But my subconscious seems to have hit back, though somewhat inartistically. A few months ago my husband had some acutely painful boils in his ears, and the other day he showed me a slight roughness on his chin. Did I think it might be an incipient boil? I said, 'No', for it seemed no more than a little roughness due to sun and salt sea air, and I at once forgot it. The next morning he woke me as usual before going into the bathroom to shave, but to my shame I fell asleep again instead of going down to get the breakfast. Shortly afterwards his return from the bathroom awakened me from a dream that he had an enormous boil on his face and, as I came to, inside my head I heard an Order: 'Ask him if he has just been looking at his spot.' I did. He had.

It is only too obvious that chance or subconscious fear on my part of a renewal of his very painful boils is the probable explanation of my dream. At the same time, I cannot put it beyond my subconscious to have used the combination of the narrow range of time, my sleepy state and my husband's very natural emotional recoil from the idea of more boils to give me a hint not to ignore possible E S P in dreams. If my conjecture is right that a whole combination of circumstances have to be favourable before E S P can emerge, the subconscious can only demonstrate its existence when this happens. J. W. Dunne comments of his precognitive dreams that whatever it was that caused them seemed to have to wait years for suitable opportunities.[2] He also describes a series of precognitive dreams of which some had characteristics which resembled mine and were equally trivial.[3] It seems to be the circumstances as much as the material which enable E S P to emerge.

[2] J. W. Dunne, *Intrusions* (Faber, 1945), p. 115.
[3] *Experiment with Time* (Faber, 1934), Chapter VIII.

CHAPTER XVI

Attempts to Exercise ESP: Hand-reading

Paradoxically, when I first began to use what looked like ESP for reading hands, I did not know what I was doing. To read hands at all, of course, is far beyond the pale of orthodoxy. How far I have just been reminded, somewhat to my amusement, by a learned medical practitioner of an art, hypnosis, which itself has but lately crept within that pale. This is how he began a lecture on the subject: 'Once upon a time hypnosis used to be classed with superstitions like poltergeists and palmistry and that sort of thing . . .'[1]

That sort of thing doubtless included the many traditional methods of seeking for information *via* purported ESP; from cards or crystals, ouija boards or tealeaves, or, if you are a tribal medicine man, entrails or bones. Tibetan Lamas are reported to stare at stones which have wavy lines or cracks on them, until eventually they see these as Chinese characters which bring them information. Anything, in fact, appears to do. Silly and superstitious enough no doubt—but the trouble is, it seems to work more often than we would like. If so, why?

It jumps to the eye that such procedures all involve factors which seem to encourage ESP. To begin with, self-consciousness is reduced, for every one of them enables the experient to dramatize to himself that the information he gets is being purveyed to him from the outside. The seers of old believed themselves to be possessed by gods or familiar non-human spirits; so, today, do devotees of Voodoo and similar rites; and nearer home spiritualist mediums suppose themselves to be controlled by

[1] Since writing this chapter a report has appeared in *The Times* for November 12th, 1962, that a research project, which may ultimately enable doctors to foretell something of a baby's probable medical history from its palm prints, is being started by an eminent paediatrician with the backing of the Sheffield Regional Hospital Board. Experts, says the report, have already proved that certain inherited illnesses produce characteristic signs on the palm. To what extent time will justify this remains to be seen, but it is a different procedure from using a hand as a focal point to encourage the emergence of ESP.

discarnate human beings. In each case all the experient has to
do is to get his conscious mind, whose activity tends to inhibit
the emergence of subconscious material, out of the way. There
are a number of means of doing this. One is to wait passively in
quiet surroundings for dissociation to take place. Others are
group ritual, invocations, or the frenzied dancing of shamans or
Voodoo devotees. But in every case the object is the same: dissociation.

Next, in all such procedures, the experient is not trying to
exercise ESP for its own sake; he is simply trying to find out something; his mind is not on the process itself. Also he is pleasantly
free from responsibility. He is only the postman; if the news is
bad, it is not his fault. Finally, his audience is seldom hostile or
ultra-critical, on the watch, as investigators must be, for any possible means by which he may be deceiving them. Rather, it will
have its tongue hanging out for Messages to arrive in Mysterious
Fashion from Realms Unknown. When, shortly after my marriage,
I began to read hands I knew little of psychology and less of parapsychology, but I can now see that all these factors were at work
in what success I had.

The game began like this. When browsing through some books
which had belonged to my grandfather I came upon one by *Cheiro*, the 'celebrated palmist'. (What had my grandfather—a Victorian cricketing, shooting, fishing Colonel—been doing with
that?) I read it and decided to try the game 'for fun', but it never
occurred to me that ESP could be involved; I merely felt vaguely
that hand-reading might be a means of contact with people as they
really were, behind the masks. Fortune favoured me, for my
husband's transfer to diplomatic life provided a splendidly varied
clientèle ready to hand. Moreover, the game was an admirable
dinner-party alternative to bridge—I was scared of becoming a
bridge addict—far better than hours and hours of boring ritual
conversation with people whom chance, not choice, had thrown
me up against.

There was no shortage of clients once I let it be known that
I was willing to read characters from hands. Characters, not for-
tunes. Hospital life had at least revealed too much about human
suggestibility to risk frivolous chatter about the future, unless it
could be attributed to present tendencies. It was extraordinary

how even the most cynical and astute seemed to delight in letting down the mask and 'being themselves' to someone who appeared —if I made a lucky opening gambit—to know something of what 'themselves' were like already.

I soon found that the game had the fun of a detective story. At first my idea of what to expect was vague. It seemed only commonsense that the shape, texture and gestures of a hand must indicate certain characteristics. A red solid hand with stiff fingers must surely symbolize a different kind of person from a pale flabby hand with limp fingers. Folded fingers suggested a different approach to life from those flung wide apart. And so on. At first I was snobbishly resistant to the idea that lines in the palm could indicate mental or emotional states. It was too ridiculous—why should line A be linked with the 'heart' and line B with the 'head'?—but I felt instinctively that the way to success was to suspend criticism. I must dramatize to myself that all this did mean something. Right away I got a warning against a snobbish attitude to traditional practices even here. Soon after I had read *Cheiro* a friend asked my advice about her housemaid who had told her in confidence that there was insanity in her family and she knew that one day she too would 'go mad'. Poor little girl. That was the sort of thing to wake up Orders, and they did not hesitate. 'Look at her hand,' they said.

I asked to do so on the excuse that I was trying to learn the game from every available hand. She agreed at once and what I saw astonished me. It was the traditional palmist's configuration for mental trouble. But—it was on her left hand only. Nonsense or not, hypocrisy or not, chance coincidence or not, the way to help was clear. Like any medicine man, I pronounced with authority that there had been mental trouble in her family, but most fortunately it had entirely passed her by. She looked as if the Pythia had spoken, became a different person, and lived happy ever after. So that, I thought, is what suggestion dressed up as the occult can do; for she would not, I am sure, have taken the least notice had I said the same thing as from myself. Moreover, should I have said it with the same conviction had I not dramatized to myself that the lines would tell the truth? I do not think so.

After that I could not in honesty ignore the lines, but I did make friends with the head of the fingerprint department of Scotland Yard and took him some unnamed fingerprints—they were my family's—to see what he would make of them. What he made put an end to my snobbish inhibitions. If he could get all that from a mere fingertip, why should the lines not be instructive too even though I could not see any reason for it? But it seemed to make sense to translate the particular into the general. When, for instance, the book said a certain configuration meant divorce, I translated this into 'a bad jolt'. And so on.

The technique which evolved itself was to try and read a pair of hands as one would an absorbing book, staring at them quietly, forgetting all else, feeling for the balance of relationship between colour, shape, texture, line-pattern and so on. But eventually, though not always, something quite different began to happen, something which I had not expected. Quiet concentration on a hand could lead to a kind of upwelling of specific information which usually concerned the basic attitudes, worries or longings of its owner, and which, I would discover later, occasionally appeared to have been precognitive. For example, in 1938, on a voyage across the Atlantic, I met William Armstrong, a well-known figure in the theatre, and he let me look at his hands. I did not see him again until ten years later when he told me that everything I had prophesied had come true. This startled me for, as I said, I did not go in for prophecy and was always surprised when told I had indulged in it. I was also inclined to forget most readings very quickly. These two points may suggest an occasional mild degree of dissociation.

Some of my hits I doubt if Sherlock Holmes himself could have deduced from sensory clues, but presumably the whole lot could have occurred by chance. As experient I find chance less probable than ESP because of the manner in which the impressions appeared in my mind. I also doubt if they would have appeared at all without my previous concentration on the hands. The fact that this concentration seemed to pass over insensibly into ESP was what first made me wonder whether we are right to assume an iron curtain between the two types of perception. They may merge into one another, as was hinted at by the resemblance between Gilbert Murray's description of his own telepathy and Keats' comments on imagination. If that is so, for experimenters to set experients to guess through boring packs of cards without any preliminary deductive warming-up may not always be the best method of inducing E S P.

Talk about procedure in hand-reading is dull without any illustrations, but too many descriptions of the characters and problems of unknown people, although they might help to lessen suspicion of chance bull's-eyes, would be dull too. Nor is what one sees in a hand always public property. Nor, again, can one ever be sure at what point deduction passes over into E S P—if it does—but I am inclined to give E S P the benefit of the doubt when what I see in the hand of a person I have met for the first time seems to go beyond deduction, and when it impresses him and is also the opposite from what I expect. Here are a couple of instances, dating, for discretion's sake, from before the last war.

In the early days of the Spanish Republic our ambassadress summoned me to help entertain the new Spanish Ambassador whom, her Toryism being cobalt blue, she clearly looked upon as a Dangerous Red. So far I had met no revolutionaries and hoped for a chance to look at his hand, for although I had every sympathy with his party, I felt that he might want to change human nature a little faster than it could take and I wondered if and how this would show. At least I did not doubt for a moment that his interest would lie in the future rather than the past.

The Dangerous Red turned out to be a gentle delightful man with whom I got on excellently, and his hands were soon spread out before me. To my astonishment, one impression only flooded my mind. Here was no revolutionary, but a man whose whole interest was centred in the past—the past—the past. But to say so would scarcely be good manners. However, the unexpected impression was so intriguing that manners went by the board, I said what I saw, and he looked delighted. 'You're entirely right,' he said, 'I'm a Professor of History. My period is the sixteenth century. I'm not at all interested in anything else.'

Poor little man. He seemed quite bewildered at having been swirled by the currents of revolution into those worldly gilded halls.

And here is a similar impression, equally unexpected but in reverse. My host at dinner asked me to look at the hand of a small, quiet man, a Mr Freeman. He was in business in New York and had a French wife. At first my mind was a blank; there seemed nothing to say about so undramatic a person. Then gradually it became filled with a great longing to escape at all costs from the overwhelming past. This really seemed exaggerated. How could that quiet little man have an overwhelming past? The word was too big. However, I had to say something—if one does not people are inclined to imagine that one sees they are about to die within five minutes. So I said it. He looked at me gravely, answered, 'You are quite right,' and changed the subject. Later I found out who he was: a member of one of the most famous and ill-fated of European royal houses. No wonder he had changed his name to Mr Freeman.

That then is the kind of pattern which I take as possibly suggestive of ESP—when I surprise myself, and when what I say seems to strike a deep chord in my client. Long before I had heard of psychosomatic medicine, for instance, I was much surprised at saying to a prosperous pink and white young stranger that I thought he had eczema on account of his bad relations with his mother. 'I do,' he replied, 'it's round my waist. And my relations with my mother couldn't be worse.' I was again surprised to find myself saying to another stranger at a dinner party that his work was his life and that even his wife and children were but shadows to him. 'You are right,' he said with emphasis, 'I do research. It is my whole life. Nothing else matters.'

I am still wondering how the hand-reader gets his information. Is it from the hands themselves? Or does sitting quietly with their owners facilitate telepathic contact with their hidden preoccupations; is the client's role that of the agent in spontaneous telepathy? As a rule I could feel that emotionally people came at least half-way to meet me, but occasionally someone who was clearly determined never to be caught by that sort of clap-trap would challenge me to read his hands and then do an excellent imitation of a marble statue at the North Pole. With such people I have never got beyond elementary rational deduction, no doubt, they would say, because they were careful not to give anything away. (It is quite extraordinary, incidentally, what even the most astute people will give away, and were one dishonest one could often impress Mr X by reading something in his hand at 9.15

that he had mentioned himself at 8.45 and then forgotten.) But from the experient's point of view the marble statue attitude has an odd effect. It is as if a kind of smog flowed into one's mind, and forced it, as a physical smog may force a car, to chug slowly and uncomfortably to a stop. It is not in physics alone that the observer modifies the phenomenon.

CHAPTER XVII

Further Attempts

When first I began reading hands I did not realize that I was trying to use E S P, and even when this seemed possible I thought little about it. I was too interested in *what* I was trying to find out to bother about *how* I found it. This was probably helpful as it avoided the attempt to exercise E S P for its own sake in cold blood, which I always find inhibiting.

I have already recorded two incidents in my youth when I tried to listen in on a friend's meditation and appeared to succeed. Conditions at the time happened to suit me. I was not self-conscious; it did not matter if I failed; the room was quiet; I was fond of the agent; and I had a motive—curiosity. On those occasions the subjects of his meditation were presented to me in two different ways: I seemed to 'live' the first and hear the second verbally inside my mind. In 1928, in response to a sudden impulse, I had a somewhat similar experience; but this time, as with the purported Vivian, I got nothing formulated, merely an attitude of mind. Conditions were much the same as before: I was carefree, quiet and alone, devoted to the agent and interested in what he was doing.

The children and I were staying with the Gilbert Murrays on Boars' Hill until the baby was old enough to travel to Turkey, where my husband had gone as British Military Attaché. It was a blissful summer. I had never before had close and prolonged contact with a man of Gilbert's stature—charitable, immensely learned, witty and wise. He could also be as childish as I was, and how he made me laugh. But there was one subject I found it kinder to keep clear of—E S P. He wished it did not exist; it clashed with his philosophy. Moreover, so he told me many years later, he felt that to be accused of 'that sort of thing' would prevent his being taken seriously on other matters. A nice sidelight on our mental climate.

One shining summer morning I wandered down the garden and stretched myself out on the hillside in the sun. Birds twittered, insects hummed, the air was filled with the scent of flowers and new-mown grass—I was happy. After mulling over some recent remarks of Gilbert's I wondered idly, 'What is he working at this morning?' And then, 'Let's try and find out.'

It was easy enough to stop the wheels of thought in that sunny Elysium, and soon there floated into my empty mind an awareness —without images—of Gilbert gazing, rapt and motionless, into a deep but translucent well. Odd, I thought vaguely, that a well should be so light and clear. After a time—it was about the middle of the morning—this feeling of motionless contemplation was replaced by its opposite, intense outgoing activity. It was as if he had become a central point from which a singing silver wind swept out and around the world, as ripples sweep out from a stone thrown into a pool. These mixed visual and auditory images sound very silly and are also misleading, for I neither saw nor heard in the ordinary sense. And yet, what others are there? All images are based on sensory perceptions. These, as I said, gave me no more than Gilbert's attitude of mind, not the content of his thought. I seemed to know how he was thinking, I did not know about what.

I was far too shy to mention this little escapade to him, but I did ask casually at luncheon what he had been doing that morning. At first, he replied, he had been trying to sink himself into the mental climate in which Greek poetry was written, and then about eleven o'clock he had switched over to work for the League of Nations Union.

It would practically be the duty of an investigator who was seeking for evidence of E S P to dismiss my impressions as due to 'pure imagination'. After all I knew Gilbert was translating Greek drama and I knew how passionately he worked for the League. But the experient has to ask: if it was only imagination, why the limited awareness? Why did I not formulate what I imagined, as I can so very easily do? Whether it is foolish or not, I have to admit that to me this experience was one more almost frightening example of the possible potency of a vigorous mind, even when unaccompanied by action. That singing wind seemed to be carrying thoughts of shining charity round the world. Supposing it had been hate?

My experience in the Murrays' garden tallied with what I

might have expected. The one which follows did not. This time I became aware of something quite different; a string of facts about a man whose name I had not been given. That is one of the oddities about E S P-type experiences. Why does one sometimes get facts, at others emotions, or sensations, or merely the type and quality of thought or situation, unformulated?

The incident took place in the 1950s. A friend came in for a drink and talked about E S P. Then, laughing, he shoved an envelope into my hand and challenged me to tell him something about the writer. 'But I don't do that sort of thing,' I exclaimed.

'Oh, come on,' he said. 'At least tell me whether it's a man or a woman.'

Never being able to resist a challenge I glanced at the envelope. This was easy. The writing was forward-sloping and shaky. An old woman, of course. But as I was about to say so, some other part of me said, 'No. It's a man, younger, and very much of a homosexual.'

To imagine a less probable friend for my questioner was difficult; but I heard myself saying what I felt and adding a number of details about the writer's taste in furniture, decoration and what not. Then I thought, 'Why, this is crazy,' and stopped, saying, 'Sorry, I'm talking nonsense.'

To my surprise my questioner was shaking with laughter. 'Go on,' he said. 'You haven't put a foot wrong yet.'

That sent my morale sky-high and it may have been elation that enabled me to take a further step. If the previous items were not all chance hits the simplest hypothesis is that I picked them up telepathically from my friend. But the item I gave next he did not know. It also reached me in a different manner, *as if* an instruction came inside my mind from someone else. (I do not say that it did.) It was worded as an Order, 'Say that he likes budgerigars.'[1] I did so and added, 'Does he?'

'I don't know,' said my friend. But next day he telephoned that a post card had just come from the writer of the envelope saying that he had spent the previous afternoon buying cages for his new budgerigars.

Chance apart, how did I get the item which my friend did not

[1] The things he liked were not birds but I have to disguise details.

know? By making subconscious contact with the writer *via* him? Or *via* the envelope itself?[2] Or could I have precognized the subsequent telephone call? Such speculation seems idle enough at this stage, but merely to collect facts, facts and more facts, without casting round, however tentatively, for hints as to what is behind them, is like a squirrel collecting nuts which he does not intend to eat.

In my final example of attempted E S P I cast myself for the role of agent, with my husband as experient. If the correspondence was not a chance one it may contain a clue that expectation can affect the manner in which a telepathic signal will emerge, for I tried to make my husband see me and instead he heard me.

I did the experiment, one I had never thought of before, on the spur of the moment. I had gone to a dinner to hear a hypnotist describe his method of work, but as soon as he began I felt pretty sure that most of the audience, including myself, already knew what he was going to say. The light was dim, my armchair soft, and the speaker's gentle murmur about relaxation extremely soothing. 'Could anything,' I thought, 'be more conducive to dissociation. How can I use it?' Then came an idea: 'I'll go and visit my husband mentally.'

It seemed an ideal occasion, for he had said he was tired and would go to bed after dinner and look at the Ballet Rambert on television; so I knew where to picture myself. Also, if he did get anything, I could use the programme to check the time. Having made my plan I blotted out my surroundings, pictured myself in my husband's room and said to him mentally, 'Frank, I'm here, I'm here with you. Do you see me?' Then I looked at my watch. The time was three minutes to ten.

I could hardly wait to see if he would mention my visit, but when I got home, alas, he was almost asleep and only answered my persistent inquiries as to how he had passed the evening by patient but definitely bored grunts. However, I was so much afraid that if he had had any impression about me he would have for-

[2] There is some more or less anecdotal evidence that this can be done, though I have not seen it firsthand. An often reported case is given by Dr Osty in *Supernormal Faculties in Man* (Methuen, 1932), p. 104. He gave a sensitive, Madame Morel, a scarf belonging to a man who had vanished. When holding it she traced his dead body, mentally, to a remote place in a wood, where it was then sought for and found.

gotten it in the morning—I knew he would not have thought it particularly interesting—that the ferret got the better of wifely devotion and I cruelly woke him up to say that I had tried to visit him and had hoped he would mention it first.

'Well, you seem to have succeeded,' he said resignedly, 'for I heard you unlock the front door and come upstairs and go into the kitchen. I thumped three times as I thought you'd like to see the end of the Ballet, but you took no notice. I was surprised and thumped again, but as you apparently didn't want to come up, I left it at that.' (My husband's room is over the kitchen and three thumps on the floor are his usual summons to me, 'Come quickly.' Hence his surprise when I did not.)

'What time was that?' I asked.

'Just before the ten o'clock news.'

It was not until I began to write this chapter that I saw a plausible reason why, if that was a case of E S P, he should have heard rather than seen me. During the eleven years we had been in our house both our sons and I had often dined out without him, but it was a family joke that, however softly we crept in, we always woke him up. That, we told him, made us feel horribly guilty. On this occasion he insisted that, as usual, he had clearly heard the sounds of my return, turning the key in the lock, walking upstairs, going into the kitchen and so on. (I always do this when I come in, to tidy up and lay the breakfast.) And once one has thought of it, it seems natural that his impression of my return, even if it was telepathic, would emerge as an auditory hallucination of the way I normally do so, rather than as a visual one, which would not make sense to him if he had not heard me come in.

As against all this I hasten to add that our house, which is in Chesham Street, cannot be far from the underground river which runs from Knightsbridge to the Thames, passing over Sloane Square Station in a pipe. It has been pointed out by some psychical researchers than an increased flow of underground water after rain can sometimes cause a building above it to creak, and it could therefore be argued that our house happened to creak several times at the exact moment when I was picturing myself at home, and that my husband simply mistook its creaks for the sounds of my entry. As against this he has never noticed the house creaking on any other occasion—and there is very little he fails to notice.

I have given this incident in some detail because it once more illustrates the difference of approach between the investigator seeking for evidence of E S P and the experient looking for clues as to how it works. The investigator would say, very rightly, 'Nonsense! There's not a leg to stand on. The husband did not mention his experience until his wife told him what she had done, and even then his impression did not tally exactly with her thought.' The experient says, 'Is the fact that the impression did not tally exactly with the agent's thought, but did with her general intention, a clue to the mode of operation of E S P?'

It would also be reasonable for an investigator to say, 'Well, if you think you visited your husband once, intentionally, why not do it again for me?' To which all I can answer is, 'The conditions would not be the same. I should not feel spontaneous or carefree, but self-conscious—watched. And my own critical mind would also be turned on what I was doing, which for me usually seems to knock out extra-sensory type activities.'

This sounds pretty feeble, but it may be true, at least for most of us; though there are a few star performers, like Dr Soal's remarkable card-guessing subjects, who appear to thrive on an ultra-critical audience. Unfortunately they are very thin on the ground.

CHAPTER XVIII

The Singing

Here are two quotations from two well known physicists. 'Perhaps there do indeed exist universes interpenetrating with ours; perhaps of a high complexity; perhaps containing their own forms of awareness; constructed out of other particles and other interactions than those we know now, but awaiting discovery through some common but elusive interaction that we have yet to spot. It is not the physicist's job to make this sort of speculation, but today, when we are so much less sure of the natural world than we were two decades ago, he can at least license it.'[1]

'When we thought we were studying an external world our data were still our observations; the world was an inference from them.'[2]

I have written down these remarks to encourage myself in the conjecture that human beings may sometimes experience common elusive interactions without spotting them, simply because their attention is concentrated on more obvious things. And at this point I need a good deal of encouragement. So far, apart from my 'split' and my meeting with the purported Vivian, the experiences I have recorded at least corresponded to some extent with outer events. Those to come do not all reach even that standard of respectability. In fact the only conventional excuse for not scrapping the lot is that a few were shared with another person—and even that could be looked upon as due to suggestion.

Why then, is the obvious question, do you choose to inflict these vague imaginings on other people? I gave my only answer to this at the beginning of Chapter XIII—that in the end my vague imaginings have driven me to the conclusion that even when they do not know it men and women are reacting all the time to elements in their surroundings which are not perceptible *via* the known senses. If that is so, it may sometimes help to ex-

[1] Denys H. Wilkinson, F.R.S., 'Matter and Sub-matter', *The Listener*, July 21st, 1960, p. 96.
[2] Sir Herbert Dingle, *The Scientific Adventure* (Pitman, 1952), p. 261.

plain otherwise puzzling human moods and behaviour. But whether it is so or not will never be discovered unless some of those who are faintly conscious of such reactions are prepared to risk the danger of being thought a fool by saying so.

The most constant of these experiences is what, for want of a better term, I call the Singing. Years ago I tried several times to write down a description of this curious phenomenon, for I was too shy to talk about it. But each attempt was vaguer, sillier and more misleading than the last. I tore them all up in disgust.

Now I have come to know four other people who seem to have heard this Singing, two of them well-known authors in whose writings I found it obliquely referred to. For both of them it accompanied a moment of revelation following a bad shock. For neither was it an everyday experience. As an experient I suspect that this may be because they have not discovered the knack of switching their everyday attention towards it. I do not think I should have done so, but for marrying a man who did not inhibit me, and sojourning for a time, however recalcitrantly, among the Cultists.

If some people can hear the Singing, then surely so can others; and one more attempt to describe it may be worth while. But to take what I say about it literally would be like taking the description of a performance of the *Appassionata* sonata as fiery to mean that performer and piano had gone up in flames.

The Singing seems to tell me something about my environment. It is best described as a kind of continuous vibrant inner *quasi*-sound, to which the nearest outer analogy is the noise induced by pressing a seashell against the ear, or perhaps the hum of a distant dynamo. This sounds like tinnitus to anyone else, but to the experient it does not appear to be heard by the ear or to be exactly located. Rather, like light, it pervades the whole atmosphere, though it is most clearly perceptible in a wide arc above and behind the head. And—I cannot explain what I mean by this —it does not appear to ring through outer space, yet neither is it far 'in'. The right word again may be borderline, if, as I most imprudently venture to suspect, there is no sharp barrier between sensory and extra-sensory phenomena.

To hear the Singing in normal circumstances needs a deliberate switch of attention, for it is very delicate. By listening carefully I can just do so, sometimes, through normal conversation, and now I can hear it with an effort through the tapping of my type-writer. But I cannot pay attention to it through, say, the hubbub of a cocktail party or the blast of a road drill. On the other hand, there are places where it will force itself on one's attention. It makes the silence live. Indeed, at times I think of it as the hum of life, for it is always louder when life of any kind feels more intense. The only time I have failed to hear it, though I listened intently, was while waiting for a train late at night in Hampstead Tube Station. I was alone on the platform. The silence was dead.

At one time the sceptic in me said, 'Imagination again. You are simply misinterpreting a physical process, just as you once misinterpreted your heart-beats as a witch's footsteps.' But I suspect the sceptic is wrong for it is easy to differentiate the Singing from physical awareness of the heart's activity—they both go on simultaneously—and also from the semi-sound I used to hear in my ears when the war, work and the menopause had sent my blood pressure sky high. Another possibility is that the Singing is a hallucination, self-created to convey subconscious apprehensions to the conscious mind; but I cannot say it seems like that. It seems like the normal result of some type of signal, in the same sense that hearing is the normal result of sound waves in the ear.

It was good to be able to speak of the Singing to my husband without embarrassment and even better to learn that he could hear it too—though it would no more have occurred to him to volunteer this fact than to say that he could see. We both observe its increase on the same occasions. 'The Singing is very strong here,' he will comment just as I am about to say the same.

It is far more evident in some places than in others; particularly so in a quiet wood, for instance, or on a moor or a mountain—clean wild places unspoilt by man. It is also clear in, say, a church or a college library, places where thought or devotion have been intense for years; and it can ring out in an ordinary room where concentrated thought has just been going on. I test this sometimes in a mild way by saying casually—not, of course, giving the reason why—'Hullo, have you just been thinking extra hard?' The answer is always, Yes.

Although the Singing seems to differ according to its apparent origin I cannot formulate in what this difference lies. I can only say that mountain Singing conveys a different 'atmosphere' from church Singing, as an oboe conveys a different 'atmosphere' from a trumpet; but I cannot say that the quasi-sound is on a higher or lower note in the scale. And, of course, I know that I am on a mountain or in a church, so sometimes, at least, the difference may be imaginary.

Until recently I never had the courage to mention the Singing to anyone but my husband and to Theodora Bosanquet when she spoke of an equivalent experience, about which she too had always kept very quiet. But with age one gets less thin-skinned, and the other day, on impulse, and partly I must admit to watch his shocked reaction, I described it to a clever young engineer. This time the biter was bit. He replied placidly, 'Oh, yes, I hear that too in places where there have just been strong emotions.'

I know of no way to illustrate the Singing, but it may be worth while giving a few examples of its sounding a note which seemed to convey specific associations. I will take these from my apparent awareness of the Christian note because it seems odd that I should be responsive to that, having flung away from the Church in adolescence and never returned. But perhaps to have lost belief in the Church and its dogmas does not imply loss of reverence for the spiritual quality of the New Testament, and the Singing seems to be expressive of kind, of quality, not of dogma. Perhaps another way to put it is that it spreads an ambience. But none of that will mean anything to those who have not heard it.

I think that the ability to observe the Singing may date from the occasion when I appeared to react to the little figure on the Holy Crank's mantelpiece, but I am not sure of this, for in those days I had not learnt to play ornithologist to myself as goose carefully enough to note exactly the onset of an experience. Soon after that incident we went to live in an old converted barn in a Sussex village and there for the first time I became aware of the Singing on a note I labelled Christian, because it seemed to emanate from the church just over the wall. This note, once more to use an analogy, appeared to be on a different 'beam' from the influence at the Holy Crank's. There the impact was on the lower half of the body, whereas a Christian note, if strong enough, may cause a reaction in the head and heart.

I listened for the Christian note in several quiet empty churches and found that in some it would pass over into a more intense experience, as if—I repeat as if—an inner force were streaming from the altar. This impression seemed more marked in churches where the Sacrament was reserved, and I tested it in some Anglican churches before looking to see whether or not the light indicating its presence was burning before the altar. The Host, of course, is always present in a Roman Catholic church.

To a person with my agnostic outlook such an experience was disconcerting, but to deny it repeatedly would have been dishonest. And yet to put it down to suggestion or imagination was not easy. Possibly, I thought, the devotional element in the congregations was stronger than in more austerely Protestant places of worship, and this had left some kind of inner emotional imprint. However, a yet greater shock to my self-conceit was in store. Our friend Mary had asked me to go and cheer up a poor old invalid lady in Brighton, and I did so, very bored, but self-righteously resigned to listen with the best grace I could to her babble about auras and karma and the rest. Once more snobbery went before a fall. What I got was a blast of the Christian note so strong that it knocked out my power to talk, as the glare of a searchlight knocks out the power to see. I could not think where it was coming from, for it did not fit the old lady's oriental leanings, and I peeped shame-facedly behind me at the mantelpiece to see if on it there could after all be some Christian symbol. It will be seen that the sceptic in me was having a bad time.

After I had turned more than once, the old lady said rather stiffly, 'If you're looking for the time because you're bored, do please go. I should quite understand.'

As only the truth could atone for my apparent rudeness, much embarrassed I blurted it out. At least it made her afternoon. 'Why, it's my ring,' she exclaimed delightedly, 'It was blessed for me by a Christian bishop.'

I was now between the devil and the deep sea. This kind of thing did not make sense. But how could I explain it away? One could say that knowing I was in a church I imagined the Christian note, and that between the old lady and me there occurred a flash of telepathy, facilitated perhaps by my genuine efforts to feel sympathetic to her outlook although it made me prickle. But this is a record of experience and *qua* experience it did not seem like that. It seemed as if I recognized a particular type of note as one recognizes the sound of a particular instrument. I do not for a moment expect, however, that I could do this if self-conscious under test conditions.

When living in Budapest in the nineteen thirties I had a chance to check this type of experience. Although I was an unbeliever, the Archbishop kindly invited me to hear the famous Easter Saturday music in the *Matthias kirche*, the great church that towered on a rocky bastion above the Danube. When I arrived—too early— I found that a seat had been kept for me in the choir itself, and from it I could see the lamp burning quite near above the altar.

'I'm very near the Host,' I thought, 'I'll try to see if I'm still receptive to that sort of influence.' I did not suppose I was, having flung myself headlong into the sad, gay, 'eat drink and be merry for tomorrow we die' life of Hungary between the wars, which tuned in too well at the time with a dark mood of my own. As I expected I could feel no force flowing from the altar. 'There you are,' I said to myself. 'You're no longer receptive.' But another part of me replied, 'You can't feel the force because the Host is not in the church.'

'Nonsense,' I said, 'It's a Catholic church, and the altar light is shining.'

'No, it's not.'

At that I said to myself deliberately, 'Very well. The light says the Host is present. I say it is not. We will find out later who is right.' I did not have to wait long. Shortly afterwards the service began and during its course a procession came in from the vestry bearing aloft the Host. On inquiry afterwards I learnt that it is always removed from a Church on Good Friday and returned on Easter Eve. But the weakness in my test is evident. I cannot be sure that I had never read or been told of this procedure and forgotten it with my conscious mind, though not with the hidden self that apparently never forgets.

So far I have written about the Singing as such and mainly about the Christian note as being an unexpected one for me to recognize. But the Singing often conveys other 'atmospheres' and sometimes it will pass over into more formulated experiences. Of these I will give some examples in the next chapter.

Postscript

When typing a fair copy of this attempt to describe the Singing I thought what a fool—and a coward—I was to funk asking my friends if they too heard it. So I went straight away to see an intelligent and sensitive woman, the daughter of a famous lawyer and with much of his power of analysis. I had not got far with a tentative attempt to describe the experience when her face lit up. 'I know exactly what you mean,' she said, 'I hear it too, in quiet places at night—especially on a mountain. I call it the Singing.'

Then she went on to say that once, when on a mountain with her sister, the Singing had been so loud that she had summoned up courage to speak of it. 'Oh, I always hear that,' said the sister. Yet neither of them had ever mentioned it to the other.

This made my own silence seem yet more absurd. Perhaps a lot of people could hear the Singing if they only learnt to listen. I tried one or two, but they had not. Then I tried an adventurous minded scientist who also had a medical degree, and to my great delight he understood what I meant. 'I have heard it myself,' he said, 'but only once.' I have since tried one or two more, with no success. It does not seem to be a widely observed experience.

CHAPTER XIX

Non-Human Presences

I now have to tackle a difficult task—to try to describe something which may be a form of E S P when there is nothing to describe, nothing, that is, to which one can give any sensory equivalent. All I can say is that sometimes I feel aware of the presence of invisible non-human entities. I cannot describe this awareness. I cannot say why I feel they are non-human. I cannot say what in sensory terms they might look like. But I do have an impression of their nature, their quality, and of their attitude towards myself. I will give examples of three different types, the first delightful, the second malevolent and the third uplifting.

I cannot pretend that I relish making this sort of thing public. Nature mystics can get away with it, and it is easy enough for poets. Nobody turns a hair when Akenside writes that

> . . . all alone, for many a summer's day,
> I wandered through your calm recesses, led
> In silence by some powerful hand unseen.

Nobody laughs at Wordsworth for writing that an invisible Being

> . . . that is in the clouds and air
> That is in the green leaves among the groves
> Maintains a deep and reverential care
> For the unoffending creatures that he loves.

And we listen respectfully when Robert Bridges tells us that we are aware of

> . . . existences crowding
> mysterious beauties unexpanded, unrevealed
> phantasies intangible investing us closely
> hid only from our eyes by skies that will not clear
> . . . and in moments of Vision
> their unseen company is the breath of life.

But it is a very different matter for a housewife to write of meeting invisible unoffending creatures, not to mention Greater Beings, in pedestrian prose.

'What on earth do you mean, invisible?' asks any sensible person, 'Merely, I suppose, that when you come along the rabbits fly to their burrows and the beetles creep under the stones?'

And I have to reply, 'Yes, that—and more.' Very very occasionally it is 'as if' the Singing passed one on through itself to an awareness of a side of wild life beyond the usual register of the senses— or is it, rather, beyond the usual attention of 'civilized' man? At such moments it seems as if one consciousness pervades the whole of Nature and finds expression, not only through the visible trees and flowers and birds and animals, but also through myriads of invisible entities which form an inner part of the composite life of the wild.

In my colder-blooded moments, of course, when I'm busy being an investigator, I laugh at such nonsensical imaginings. Mere atavism! The primitive always sees Puck or Pan in every bush. But inwardly I know that attitude to be a suburban betrayal of perception; I know I have brushed the fringe of a group consciousness as real as my own, though one from which 'civilized' man has cut himself adrift, so that it shrinks from him as an invader, coarse, vulgar and arrogant, imperceptive and cruel.

My first experience of such apparent shrinking was on Dartmoor many years ago. Soon after our arrival at Okehampton my husband and I went out to catch the tail-end of the sunset. It was one of those evenings when the whole world holds its breath. The moor towered in shadowed purple contours between us and the sinking sun, and above it the western sky was green and gold like glacier water. Suddenly, without warning, the incredible beauty swept me through a barrier. I was no longer looking at Nature. Nature was looking at me. And she did not like what she saw. It was a strange and humbling sensation, as if numberless unoffending creatures were shrinking back offended by our invasion, and it struck me like a blow that even the windswept little tree against the skyline seemed to be leaning away from us in disgust. 'What shall we do?' I whispered to my husband. 'They loathe us. We can't gate-crash like this.'

He did not laugh at me. He too felt an intruder. So I said,

should we stand quite still and explain mentally that we came as friends, with humility, and would be grateful for permission to walk quietly on the moor? I thought too of the days when simple souls linked themselves to wild nature by the ancient magic of oak and ash and thorn.

Writing as experient, not as investigator, there is, thank goodness, no need to invoke sophisticated explanations like auto-suggestion for the astonishing experience that followed this gesture of apology. It was as if, like a wheeling flight of dunlin, all those visible and invisible creatures swung round as a unit to inspect us, and I seemed to feel their sigh of relief as they came to a group decision. We were not dangerous or cruel. Our apology was accepted. We might come on—and 'in'. At the time I did not even think it odd that the little wind-swept tree was now leaning towards us in a friendly fashion.

That experience had an unexpected aftermath. A couple of mornings later I was alone by a window facing the moor, writing letters and thinking of nothing less than its invisible inhabitants. Then I too suffered an invasion, a delightful one. It was as if, like ebullient children, a covey of little invisibles floated in at the window to say, 'Hullo!' and coax me to play with them. For a moment their visit seemed perfectly normal, but then my analytical mind got going, and at once, for me, they ceased to exist. And now I have no idea at all whether or not I had been 'conversing with things that really are'. How anyway can we know what things there really are beyond the phenomena which Eddington has described as 'peculiar to the limited imagination of the human brain', or beyond the reach of our parochial senses? A few years ago one of our greatest physicists told me to remember that had I been equipped with radar instead of eyes, when I looked at the sky I should see objects where I now saw empty space.

The unoffending creatures of the moor seemed to recoil from us in fear, but a fear that we felt we managed to overcome. I must now record an experience in which, on looking back, I feel regretfully that we may have done less well. This time we seemed to come up against entities which were not only violently hostile to us but malevolently evil as well. But were they? Now I cannot help wondering whether the fierce hate we felt so acutely may not have been due to terror because we were threatening their very existence.

We encountered them in 1927. Once more our awareness of them was imageless—simply an impression of their non-human nature and their attitude towards us. A group of old barns in a Sussex village had been converted into dwellings, very romantic but also complete with power plants and all modern conveniences, and of these my husband and I took a lease of the first one available. Our furniture arrived late one night in a howling gale and once the beds were up we flung ourselves down on them, exhausted, and slept till morning. On waking we stared at each other, thoroughly shaken. 'The baby can't possibly come here!' we said. This knowledge was in both our minds as we woke up but I cannot say how it got there for we could remember no dreams. It was the more disconcerting in that there was nothing definite to take hold of. We were simply aware of hate—that hostile invisible non-human entities belonged to the place and desperately wanted to drive us away.

I felt non-plussed and discouraged. Having signed the lease we could not afford to go elsewhere and I knew of no way of dealing with hostile entities that could be neither seen nor heard. But my husband is never at a loss. 'John,' he said (John was an ardently Christian friend), 'has been talking to me about exorcism. The obvious thing to do is to find a Christian priest and ask him to clean the place up.'

This matter-of-fact attitude cheered me. He might have been saying, 'We'll get a maid with a mop and some Jeyes' Fluid.' I thought too, 'Well, the experience may not be rational but for us it's actual enough. Why then be snobbish about people who are willing to try and deal with it, even if their methods are not mine?' So I agreed, and my husband went off exorcist hunting, to return in triumph at tea-time with a very mild little priest. He seemed a far from adequate David to cope with the bitter antagonists whose presence we had felt that morning.

After tea the priest asked for salt and water, and I went to fetch these from the kitchen at the far end of the house. Then came a shock. It was a hell's kitchen, a raging whirlpool of hate, dismay and, strongest of all, panic. I felt as if I were being battered by almost physical breakers of panic and was very tempted to turn and bolt. However, although at the time I knew nothing of systematic investigation, the instinct to test the unusual was too strong, and I took some water only, returned to the drawing-room and said casually to my husband, 'Oh dear, I've left the salt. Do get it, will you?'

He went off cheerfully, but on his return even he looked taken aback. 'Good gracious,' he said, 'that kitchen.'

After the priest had performed his ritual my husband drove him home. By now it was dark and I knew I had to try and check whether the place had really been cleaned up for the baby; not that I liked the idea for it meant turning out all the lights and sitting in each room, including the kitchen, with inner 'antennae' out. The result was astonishing. The raging hate had gone, the terror had gone, and in their place was a quiet shining peace. A greater contrast to the dark whirlpool of an hour earlier could scarcely have been imagined.

We never spoke of the dispossessed entities and a year or so later we lent the house to my sister. She is a balanced competent person—she drove an ambulance with the greatest calmness all through the blitz—but on one or two occasions she has independently located invisible presences in the same places as I have, and also in other places where she afterwards heard that there was some tradition which might account for such impressions. She told me some time after we had left the house that to go into the kitchen at night had filled her with terror. There was, she said, something quite horrible there. What then caused our sense of cleansing? Merely suggestion? Or was the cleansing effective only for us? Had we alone been insulated? Or was it temporary, as when one scrubs a floor? Or did my sister pick up, telepathically, our memory of an experience which had, in me at least, produced plenty of emotional fuel? And finally, had my husband and I had any genuine experience of something outside ourselves, or had one of us telepathically infected the other with the fruits of his or her own imagination?

To turn from that dark brush with invisible hate to the next two experiences is like escaping into the sunlight from a malodorous cave. (I think it is usually the differing emotional atmospheres of various E S P-type experiences which convince the experient that they did originate outside himself, but this is a difference which cannot be shared with an investigator.) These two experiences were both of beneficent Beings who appeared to transcend humanity, but whose concern, nevertheless, was with its welfare. Both took place in the usual conditions: I was sitting quietly, thinking of nothing particular and certainly not of beneficent Beings.

As it is possible that my mood at the time may have induced the first experience I shall give it in some detail. In 1938 my husband left the Foreign Service, having been asked by a friend to run the exports of his business, and I found myself temporarily sharing my mother's house at Sunningdale. With an active diplomatic life cut short, the children at school and most of my friends abroad, I gasped like a goldfish in an empty bowl. How to escape? What to do?

At first the cosy golf and bridge playing world of Sunningdale made friendly gestures, but I did not want to spend my life playing golf and bridge, and that prosperous world clashed too bitterly with the grey half-life on the dole which in those days was led by thousands of men and women but a few miles off. Was there any way a stray woman could help them? Do little jobs for the Labour Party perhaps? I still half hoped they might hold the keys to a kingdom where everyone would get a fair chance, and at least they were not disgustingly content with things as they were.

Sunningdale soon discovered that it had nearly taken an asp to its bosom, for it kindly offered me the chairmanship of the local Women's Conservative Association and I found myself answering—I could not resist it—'Yes, with pleasure—as long as you don't mind me voting Labour.'

Sunningdale shivered. Mrs Heywood had seemed so sensible. And here she was, politically unreliable. Who next?

Mrs Heywood, meanwhile, had taken herself off for lunch and advice to an ex-miner friend in the House of Commons. Arriving, as usual, too early, I settled down on a bench in the long entrance to Westminster Hall, relaxed, and let the world fade out. It was perhaps due to my mood—how could one help?—that I then found myself passing beyond the Singing which is very strong in such places, into the ambience, the consciousness—what words can one use?—of a profoundly wise and powerful Being who I felt was brooding over the Houses of Parliament. In that inner space he towered so high that the actual buildings seemed to be clustered about his feet. Metaphorically speaking. I was not aware of anything like feet. But I was acutely aware that his task, his deep concern, was to influence for good the deliberations of Parliament, and also that he thought in terms of long evolving patterns rather than of one particular moment in time.

As usual I could not hold this experience, nor could I repeat it next time I went to the House. Yet it moved me deeply and I longed to talk of it. But to whom? My husband was in Africa and I knew other people would only smile and say, 'Poor thing! A bit eccentric, you know.' There were, of course, the S.P.R. investigators into E S P whom I was just beginning to meet, but I had learnt very quickly that they would wince at such woolly vagueness. Then I remembered, there was one person, a saintly old man who lived alone in a wood and whom a friend had taken me to visit some months before. I had gone again several times, for his wisdom was like a magnet and I had also been intrigued by his apparent exercise of helpful E S P about a friend of mine abroad, who was in trouble and about whom I was sure he could never have heard. No, he at least would not laugh at me.

He did not. On the contrary, as soon as I arrived he began spontaneously to talk of the Angel of the House of Commons. Too startled to remember about investigation I blurted out, 'Then you have felt it too?'

He laughed. 'Of course I have,' he said.

His use of the word Angel gave me food for thought. Before modern science ruled out such things, experiences of this kind would obviously have led to a belief in Angels, Devas, or whatever you cared to call them. To what belief do they lead now?

Some years later, when waiting for my younger boy in an empty music school at Eton, I once more seemed to pass through the Singing into the ambience of a great Being. He appeared to have the school in his care and, like his fellow at Westminster, he created an atmosphere of brooding wisdom and calm. I think the most impressive part of these experiences was this sense of calm, of certainty. They were in no hurry. They knew what they were about. And they made humanity seem like flustered ants.

CHAPTER XX

Human Presences

In the last chapter I gave some examples of awareness of what seemed to be localized non-human presences. This awareness was limited. I never pictured them, even as mental images, and yet I seemed to know that some were light and gay and active, others bitterly hostile and others, again, towering, serene and immensely wise. I also felt aware of their attitudes towards me.

I now turn to apparent presences, mostly invisible, which seemed to be human. Of these my impressions have been more varied. Sometimes I have felt aware of images, sometimes not; and the same with emotions. The key to these differences may lie in the difficulty of emergence—that an extra-sensory signal has to work its way through to consciousness as and how it can, and it may arrive piecemeal, disguised or distorted, but seldom whole.

I will begin with the only exterior visual hallucination I ever had, apart from seeing Alex in Macedonia when he was in Paris. That may have been due to telepathy or simply to wish-fulfilment, but for this other figure I can find no emotional source. I saw it in 1939 when staying with my husband's brother in Johannesburg, and on another occasion my sister-in-law saw it too. This may suggest some link between it and the environment, for she and I are very different types and it is hard to imagine what common reason we could have had for creating it ourselves. But it is also hard to imagine what that link could have been, since the environment was a modern house near Johannesburg, and the figure was wearing a long white oriental looking garment.

He caught my attention by obstructing the light in the passage. At this I looked up hastily, wondering who could have broken in, for the family were at the far end of the house, and this was always locked up with care when the African servants went out to their own quarters at night. For a moment I saw the man standing quite still and apparently unaware of me. The next moment he 'was not'. I was startled and noticed a feeling of cold about my middle; but I was not afraid of him as such, and if he had been wearing ordinary clothes and had walked away I might have thought him an ordinary man. He did me one good turn. Hitherto invisible human presences had made me feel uncomfortable, just because they were invisible, but now that I had actually seen this harmless figure I was able to react to them according to what they seemed to be in themselves, happy or sad, benign or sinister, as one would react to people who were present in the ordinary physical sense.

This type of experience is what is popularly known as seeing a ghost and it is far from uncommon. A fair proportion of *Memoirs* include some such story.[1] Usually there is a tradition to account for the 'ghost', and in that case the impression could presumably have been picked up telepathically from someone who knew it. But, as I said, there appeared to be no such tradition about our figure and it did not 'fit' the environment. An explanation for it in terms of something outside ourselves is therefore hard to suggest.

My next experience, on the contrary, can quite plausibly be explained as an illusion designed to convey a subconscious opinion to the conscious mind. But whether that opinion was my own, or came to me from outside, is another matter. I do not know. I feel less diffident about describing my experience having just read of one similar recorded by Somerset Maugham in a newspaper extract from his forthcoming *Memoirs*. In both his case and mine a human head in a picture seemed to move and take notice of the onlooker. (In his case the head was that of Christ.) Maugham writes that if he were under oath in a court of law and were asked whether he had seen this happen, he would have to answer, Yes. If he then were asked whether he believed that the figure had actually moved, he would say, No, certainly not. If on

[1] A typical case is recorded by Sir Osbert Sitwell in *Left Hand, Right Hand* (Macmillan, 1945), p. 18. One of his ancestors, Sir Sitwell Sitwell, was seen, he says, quite close at the front door of his home, shortly after his death, and subsequently a face was seen looking through that door at intervals, including the day of his son's funeral, forty years later. 'These singular stories,' writes Sir Osbert, 'possess for me an especial interest because on the evening of the day on which I first heard of my mother's fatal illness, I entered the house . . . to find two friends, who were staying with me at the time, much puzzled because a tall rather indistinct figure had mounted the steps from the park and stared at them through the identical glass panels of the door; but when they opened it he was no longer anywhere to be seen.'

that he were asked to reconcile the two statements he could only shrug his shoulders and say, 'I suppose it was an optical illusion.' 'After all,' he comments, 'I was far from well and tired out. I made a note of the date on which I had this strange experience: April 20, 1958.'

In other words, though incredulous, he was impressed. But what he did not do, apparently, was to seek for a psychological reason for his illusion. When I had my illusion I was not tired out, and such a reason for it was clear enough. My picture answered a question about which I was intently pondering.

At the time it did so I had not yet got rid of another kind of illusion, that because I was fond of both A and B, they would necessarily feel drawn towards each other. This led me to take a Highland doctor, for whom I felt great affection, to visit the saintly old man who lived in the wood. Both being idealists and both apparently gifted with ESP, I assumed that they would meet with pleasure in an inner as well as an outer sense. But I could not have been more wrong. They made no contact at all. In a rather pathetic effort to do so the old man took the doctor up-stairs to see his library, and I stayed down by the fire, trying hard to work out why so unexpectedly the two seemed to live in such different inner worlds. On the wall in front of me there hung a picture of some wise man of the past, and suddenly he leant out of the frame and said, 'If those two were to meet in the sense you want them to on your level, they would lose their individuality. But they will be able to do so and yet retain it when they reach ours.'

I use the words 'he said', but this is not really accurate for although the visual experience was an outer one, he in fact conveyed his meaning in the same more immediate interior fashion as 'Julia' and 'Vivian' had conveyed theirs. I was not at all surprised. It all seemed perfectly natural, as if a wiser person than I had been kind enough to explain a puzzle to me. And what he meant also seemed perfectly clear. I suppose I must confess that to the experient side of me it still does. Immediately after his comments, as with Somerset Maugham, the picture was merely a picture as before.

I have felt very much at a loss as to how to classify my final example of a human presence. In some ways it resembled those of 'Julia' and 'Vivian', and yet, like the ghosts of tradition, it seemed to be attached to a particular place. For that reason I have put it in this chapter on localized presences. It at least illustrates the difficulty of separating experience from imagination, of avoiding the too easy jump to what may be a wrong interpretation, of separating a clue from a mirage.

At the old headquarters of the S.P.R. in Tavistock Square I used to meet an invisible man wandering about the small room at the back of the stairs and the passage which led to it. He seemed to be in a state of acute anxiety. As the house was an old one I jumped to the conclusion, without warrant, that this apparent presence must be a 'left-over' from the distant past, for I had not yet worked out that, for me at least, such 'left-overs' do not seem to be actively conscious of the present. Being a new recruit to the S.P.R. I did not want my colleagues to feel that I was a Mr Black, imagining 'ghosts' on their own premises, and so for some time I kept quiet about the poor man. But one evening when after a meeting I went to fetch my coat from the little back room, he seemed so desperately in need of help that I felt quite shaken, and could not resist blurting out to a group of senior members of the S.P.R., who were standing by the front door, that I had just met an invisible man in the little room down the passage. Out of cowardice I put it as a joke, but they did not appear to think it funny. On the contrary, they looked shocked and hastily left the house, without, I could not help observing, asking me a single question, even to check whether I had suddenly gone out of my mind or was pulling their legs. Nor could I help wondering whether this would have happened in other forms of inquiry which were still, like our inquiry into ESP, at the exploratory stage. However that might be, from the experient's point of view there was the poor worried man and there was I doing nothing to help him except to make soothing noises (interior) when we met. Much good that did him, I thought. In the end I decided to go to Edward Osborn about the problem, because he combined scientific caution with an open mind and a kind heart. (He ran the publications department for Chatham House and investigated ESP in his spare time.) To my great relief he did not treat me as a knave or a moron. He even asked a question: 'What does your man look like?'

'I don't know. But he seems to be very worried.'

'Try hard to visualize him.'

I did my best, but could only evoke a very faint mental image of a pale thin man with hollow cheeks and wispy grey hair. I put him in period clothes, but said that I was pretty sure that this was merely imagination because the house was an old one. Edward Osborn failed to find anything in its history to account for such a presence, so there seemed nothing left for me to do but try to check my experience independently. To that end, I asked the writer, Signe Toksvig, to go round the house—a large one—by herself and give me her impressions. She was sensitive to places and I could trust her. She reported an invisible presence in the ground floor passage and little back room. So far so good; if her impression was not due to chance, it might at least suggest a telepathic link with me. And then, some years later, I met an American sensitive who had visited the S.P.R., and I asked her if she had had any impressions there. 'Yes,' she said, 'I once met Whately Carington in the small back room behind the stairs. He was desperately worried about a loved relative and as a result of meeting him I was able to help her.'

Whately Carington was a scientist who had given the best part of his life to experimental research into telepathy and who had evolved a theory that it was encouraged if agent and experient both held a thought of the same object in their conscious minds. This, he felt, might act as a link between them. I had done a few little experiments for him, and it beat me why, on the wild hypothesis that he had been seeking for help, he should have tried to make contact with us in the little back room instead of in places where in life he used to meet his friends. At the same time, I had to admit that the face and physique I had so very faintly evoked were, in fact, like his, though the period clothes were wrong. Could there be a rough parallel here with the dream in which the little cat, Mitzi, appeared dressed in Spanish uniform? However, it was all very vague, and as there seemed no way of finding out for certain who my man might be, I put him out of my mind. Then, a year or two later, I wanted to look through the records of the experiments I had done for Carington and asked the secretary of the S.P.R. where they were stored. 'Here,' she replied, 'with all his experiments. They are on the shelves behind the curtain just inside the little back room.'

Any investigator could dismiss all this quite easily: a nice dose of imagination plus a nice series of coincidences. But ought an experient to do so? Or ought he to wonder whether a Carington-like impression could, so to speak, have impinged on us directly from the records themselves; subconsciously, of course, since consciously we did not know that they were there. Or ought we even to be foolhardy enough to envisage the possibility that something of Carington had survived his death and that, according to his own hypothesis when living, he had hoped that the records might be a link by means of which he might reach us to get the help he needed?

CHAPTER XXI

Picking Up the Past

Stored away in *Memoirs* and on the shelves of the S.P.R. and kindred bodies is a good deal of evidence that, on occasion, human beings appear to become aware in some extra-sensory fashion of past events connected with a particular place. And stored it seems likely to remain as long as the sophisticated condemn all such experiences as fantasy and the simple fly from them as contact with 'the walking dead'. But, looked at without assumptions, can these experiences in themselves provide any clues as to what may really be happening? If they are more than imaginary, can they, for instance, be due to telepathy from the living who know of the past events? Or can events, or the thoughts and emotions involved in them, leave a trace on objects and places? Or does the secret lie in the real nature of what used to be accepted as the ever-rolling stream of time, but which, so we are now told, does not in fact roll at all? Perhaps once more the right answer must await the right question, and that has not yet been asked.

One difficulty which often faces an experient when trying to assess his impressions of a particular place is that he knows something about its associations and in consequence finds inference and imagination hard to rule out. For that reason I give E S P the benefit of the doubt only when the experiences are quite unexpected and are found to be appropriate afterwards. In my case the type of impression varies, and unfortunately it is always incomplete. I may get a shadowy interior picture of people who were once in the place, or merely an imageless idea of them, or, again without images, I may have feelings which are afterwards found to be consonant with events which once occurred there. I will illustrate each type of impression from occasions when it has surprised me.

In 1954 I was staying with the Guy Wints near Cambridge, and one afternoon they said, 'Now we'll take you for a walk on the Great Dyke.'

For me dykes were ditches in the fens, and I jumped to the

conclusion that we were going to walk in flat country along an outsize ditch. What we did was to turn round some stacks on to a tiny path which ran between two high and thick thorn hedges up a hill. As I set foot on the path, just for a moment I felt myself surrounded by shadowy busy skin-clad figures. I can give no details for I was aware of them only fleetingly and through a mist, but the impression was so surprising that I stopped and told the Wints.

'Do you realize you've just stepped on to the Great Dyke?' said Guy.

'But a dyke's a ditch,' I protested.

'You can't see the ditch. It's behind the hedge. It was dug to continue over the hill the protection given by the marshes below. This path runs along the rampart which was made by the earth thrown up when digging it. Now tell us more about your men.'

But I could not. Anything more I said would be due to imagination. The men had vanished, and I could not bring them back. Nor could I tell whether they had anything to do with building the Dyke, as the Wints had suggested.

As usual, I tried to rake up some sensory explanation for the experience; but all I could achieve, and it seemed a bit far-fetched, was that the shape of the hill, when it appeared unexpectedly round the stacks, might have reminded me subconsciously of the South Downs and their barrows. More probable seemed telepathy from the Wints. Or, if the dyke had been dug as an urgent defensive measure, could the anxiety of the defenders have left some kind of imprint on the place? Not that I felt anxiety. I felt no emotion at all, not even fear at being surrounded by such primitive beings. I merely registered their presence in a fleeting misty way, as on a faintly lit, but, paradoxically, non-visual screen.

At least on that occasion I was aware of something about the people by whom I felt surrounded. They seemed to be wearing skins and they seemed to be busy. When staying at the British Embassy in Paris I had a similar experience several times, but this was even less specific. I simply felt, as I walked through the upstairs rooms which led into one another, that I was passing through a crowd. What kind of a crowd it was I had no idea. Later on I learnt that another visitor had also felt aware of a crowd upstairs and, in addition, had had the unpleasant visual hallucination of being ferociously glared at by a filthy ragged dishevelled woman. I have since heard that an enraged crowd was reported to have swept through the upper floors of the house during the Revolution, and to have thrown an unfortunate girl out of an upstairs window.

Very large numbers of unexpected correlations between experience and previous events would obviously be needed before the idea of any extra-sensory link between the two could be taken seriously. But experiences such as those I have mentioned have led me to wonder whether the fact that they were of emotional situations and yet lacked all emotion might tell in favour of some unknown kind of fragmentary observation of the past;[1] for imagination would presumably have served up a certain amount of appropriate emotion too.

The novelist, L. A. G. Strong, says that his own experiences have led him to the conclusion that the past can be observed, and in his autobiography he gives an example. While standing at the back of the hall in a schoolmaster friend's house he turned, having heard the front door open, to see a man enter and go into the sitting-room. On following to discover who it might be, he was astounded to find no one there. Shortly afterwards his friend came home and said, 'Hullo, you look odd!' and Strong then described the man he had seen, his brown moustache, his clothes, the music under his arm and so on. 'That,' said the friend, 'was Wilfred Alington. He was killed in 1917. He played the organ here before me. This was his room.'

About this experience Strong's comment is interesting. 'Of one thing I am certain,' he said, 'and later experience confirmed my certainty. The spirit of the dead schoolmaster was not walking. I was, so to speak, playing a gramophone record.'[2]

So much for emotionless experiences. (Strong appears to have felt no emotion on seeing the figure although he was taken aback when he found it had vanished.) My final example is very much the reverse. In the summer of 1925, long before I had learnt any-

[1] Since this was written the U.S.A. Department of Defense is said to have reported the development of a camera capable of photographing the immediate past.

[2] Summarised from a longer account in *Green Memory* (Methuen, 1957), p. 268.

thing about serious investigation of E S P, my husband went away on manœuvres and I rented a romantic Tudor cottage in the country. It stood in a delightful orchard facing south, and roses climbed over the front door which led into the long sunny chintz-curtained living-room. An idyllic place, I felt sentimentally, for our three month old baby to open his eyes on to the world. To start my idyll I sat down after dinner by the living-room door to enjoy the scented peace of the night. I did not enjoy it long. Out of the stillness, without any warning, swept a wave of fear and horror so acute that, had it not been for the baby, I would have bolted from the place like a rabbit and never returned. But there was the baby and there was no money to take it elsewhere. I had to pull myself together and face the horror. On doing so I found, to my great surprise, that it could be located. It came from the far end of the room which led into the tiny dining-room. Everywhere else was 'clean'. Problem—how to live for three months at close quarters with this horror, and yet not panic? I dared not even speak of it, for my little maid was a Londoner and already convinced that in the country a dragon lurked behind every bush. Besides, who could help me? It would be too unfair to bother my busy husband and, anyway, what could he do? (This was before the exorcism incident, and I would never have thought of that on my own.) There was only one way to cope with it. When alone at night I must never go into the dining-room or even glance into it. I must never even look towards that end of the living-room. The policy worked. But every day I dreaded the coming of night.

After I had left the cottage my mother had occasion to visit the village in which it stood, and one of its old inhabitants said to her, 'However did Mrs Heywood manage to live in that cottage?'

'Why shouldn't she?' asked my mother. 'It's a charming place.'

'Oh no, it's not,' said the old inhabitant. 'There was a soldier come home from the wars with Napoleon and he murdered his wife in the little room beyond the living-room. It's been terribly haunted ever since!'

'So that was it,' I thought, when she told me of this conversation. 'A murder!' How exactly it fitted the horror and panic that had invaded me. But whether the invasion came from the place itself, or telepathically from the local villagers, or whether I was for a while displaced in time, or even made contact with the memories of discarnate persons, I cannot tell.

This somewhat macabre experience makes a fitting end to my string of anecdotes, for it illustrates rather well the great gulf between experients and investigators who are seeking for evidence of E S P. What, after all, is there in such a story for the investigator? That I sat alone in the dark in an old cottage and felt frightened. 'Natural enough,' he would say, 'in an obviously over-imaginative young woman.'

And if I protested, 'But I did locate the exact spot where the murder was said to be committed.'

'Just so. Said to be. But where is your evidence that it was?' Which is where we came in.

CHAPTER XXII

How Can One Talk About ESP?

In the late nineteen forties Dr Eric Strauss, who was then head of the psychiatric department at Barts, asked me to have a drink with him at his flat, and there for the first time I met the medium, Mrs Osborn Leonard, a remarkable woman who managed to combine childlike faith and great integrity with an exceptional talent for ESP. In those days I kept quiet about my trivial experiences and Dr Strauss knew nothing of them. Nor certainly did Mrs Leonard. He left us on the sofa while he went to fetch the drinks, and after a moment Mrs Leonard turned to me and said casually, 'I see you do what I do. But I put it out there.' She waved a hand. 'You do it direct.'

I was as taken aback as if Schnabel had welcomed me as a colleague, but mulling over her remark afterwards brought some characteristics of my own ESP-type flickers into better focus. In the far past Mary and other sensitives had also said to me, 'You can do what we do. Why do you pretend you can't?'; but since they did not add, 'We put it out there. You do it direct,' I did not believe them. I thought they were laughing at me. After all I very seldom indulged, as they did, in dramatic exterior hallucinations or even in interior visions. As a rule the best I could do was a simple kind of sporadic 'knowing', and obedience to Orders.

Much of all that I certainly did not think of as possible ESP. Indeed, when young I had assumed that everyone experienced this 'knowing', just as everyone saw the sun and heard the birds, and I would be puzzled and even angry when they butted their heads against obvious walls or thought highly of people like the snaky parlourmaid. Later, though but dimly—it was scarcely formulated—I came to realize that some people seemed to lack the 'knowing', while others, like my husband and Mary, would experience it on occasions when I did not. Later still, I came to wonder whether we do not often react to it even when we do not know we 'know'. This, as I said earlier, could apply in particular to artistically gifted people and might account for their frequent excessive sensibility.

My meeting with the purported Vivian made sense in terms of Mrs Leonard's remark, for it contained both kinds of experience. First I participated in an imageless fashion in the quality of his new situation, although, as he said, I had no concepts for it, and afterwards that situation was symbolized 'out there'—though still inside my mind—by white wings flying in a blue sky. (Had I been simple and unintrospective, I might not have noticed the first part of the experience and could then have believed that I had actually seen Vivian flying to heaven with angel's wings.)

There are two degrees of 'out-thereness': images, representative or symbolic, inside one's mind, and—yet more 'out there'—exterior hallucinations. But these can be symbolic too. At the beginning of our post-war family crisis I lay down on our tennis court to force myself to look the fact in the face that my husband and I were dead tired, no longer young, and might shortly have no income. As I did so, in the sky beyond the surrounding trees there loomed up a vast ominous black hand. Then it moved downward towards me, very slow and menacing, its fingers contracted like the claws of a bird of prey. It was about, I knew, to seize and crunch me to pieces. At the last moment, just as it was reaching me—I was paralysed with terror—it dissolved very gently into a cloud of harmless smoke, and in a few moments the sky was clear and blue once more. When I had pulled my shaking self together I tried to work out what it might mean—having learnt by experience that that sort of thing does not happen for nothing —and came to the conclusion that it might be a symbol that we should nearly go under. But not quite. That was in fact how things turned out.

One does not know why ESP and other subconscious knowledge emerges in the same person on different occasions in different ways, or why some people incline towards one way and some to another. When rising thirteen our younger son, who takes ESP for granted, made a casual comment which suggested that degrees of 'out-thereness' originated in himself and were merely a matter of convenience. He had won a mathematical scholarship and his second report thereafter contained a lament from his two mathematics masters that they had 'besought him to tell them how he did his problems'.

'Did you tell them?' I asked him.

'No.' He never used two words where one would do.

I was intrigued. 'How do you do them?'

'Oh,' indifferently, 'I read the problem and then I see the answer.'

'Where do you see it?'

'Inside my head. I can put it out there'—he waved his hand at the blank wall—'but it's not worth the trouble.'

I made no comment and he went on to talk of serious matters like model aeroplanes.

Preference for one form or another of emergence does not seem to depend on competence or sophistication. Swedenborg, who was a genius in mundane affairs, seems to have 'seen' his purported discarnate acquaintances 'out there' in an inner space; and the efficient Mrs Willett (Coombe-Tennant)—she was the British Government's first woman delegate to the League of Nations at Geneva—although she sometimes 'saw' her 'communicators', also wrote of them, 'I get no impressions of appearance, only character. . . . It is as minds and character that they are real to me.'

This describes my own imageless awareness of the living Alex's presence when he came to London after we had broken apart, of Gilbert Murray working in his study, and of what appeared to be my discarnate friends. But then on another occasion I saw Alex 'out there' as a visual hallucination against my normal sensory environment.

One obviously hesitates to compare the trivial E S P-type experiences of ordinary people with those of great men, much less with something quite other—though it still seems to be extra-sensory—mystical experience. Yet great men and saints share the use of eyes and ears with ordinary people, and the process, though not the content, of their extra-sensory perceptions may be the same in all of them. How, for instance, to take three very different examples, did Socrates experience his Daemon, Stevenson his Brownies and Elijah his still small voice? And what did St Teresa mean when she classified her experiences into corporeal or sensorial visions; imaginative visions perceived by the soul; and visions and locutions which lacked any kind of image? Although the content of these processes was of a higher order, could they still, as processes, be equivalent to those experienced by ordinary people; exterior hallucinations seen against a sensory background, interior visual images, and direct imageless awareness, or even participation?

I am acutely aware how open to criticism is that kind of vague speculation, but it seems to fall within the role of experient, and in this subject, as Professor Price has remarked, even investigators must not be afraid of talking nonsense. Although in another context, Nils Bohr has put his finger on a very real difficulty which faces the experient who tries to be articulate: that the part of the self which is, so to speak, in focus during an ESP-type experience is not the part which later tries to analyse it. Consciousness switches from one type of vision to another, and this means that even within the experient subsequent thought about his experience is nearly always from the outside. Switches of consciousness may be experienced by more people than is commonly realized, because they prefer not to mention them. One kind of switch that is not infrequent and is more or less respectable is a sudden enhancement of vision, when what is seen becomes intensely beautiful and significant. In the middle 1950s I was walking through Eaton Square and stopped to look at a forsythia bush whose buds were beginning to burst. As I stared at it, tears of awe and ecstasy rolled down my cheeks. The beauty, the glory of that burgeoning golden life were almost too great to be borne. Last spring I again happened to walk across the Square when the forsythia was breaking into bud. This time all I saw was—yellow forsythia. Try as I would, the vision would not come back. So now I can only describe it from the outside. When the glass is dark one does not know how to clear it.

This incident brought home to me once more how hard it must be for people who have never experienced even minor changes of consciousness, or trivial ESP, much less mystical apprehensions, to realize that ordinary language is about as good a tool to describe them as a kitchen knife to dissect a cell. I doubt if even the greatest poet could convey the effect of those little forsythia buds to a person who had never felt anything like it. 'It's impossible to say just what I mean,' said Mr Prufrock.

The experient is also hampered because the words he is sometimes driven to use *faute de mieux* have technical meanings. It is legitimate, for instance, to speak of radiant smiles or a vibrant voice; but if an experient mutters about E S P-type 'radiations' or 'vibrations', investigators very naturally wince, even if they have just come from a discussion on pregnant liquor or excited atoms. Here, once more, I am uncomfortably astride the fence. I too wince when experients talk soulfully about 'Higher Vibrations', or fling around such obviously specific words as 'radio-active' with the bland assurance of ignorance, or take themselves and their wondrous visions so portentously that less aspiring experients run to P. G. Wodehouse for relief. At the same time ornithologists do not give up the study of geese because they dislike their honk; and it is a hard job to explain one kind of experience in terms of another. Moreover, the investigator does not always know why a particular word is chosen. Is, for instance, the widespread use of the tiresome word vibration due to a fashion set by Madame Blavatsky; or is it sometimes a genuine attempt to describe an impression that something in the surroundings is in constant motion, rather than static? This would seem true of a piece of lead, could it be observed at atomic level, and it can apply to the whole world in the eyes of persons whose vision has been distorted by a hallucinogen, such as mescalin or LSD25 or psylocybin. Would the word emanation better convey what the experient is trying to express? And if he used it, how should we react?

Investigators who have taken a hallucinogen come nearer to understanding the language problem faced by experients, and the fluid fleeting nature of hallucinogenic visions also helps them to understand another difficulty; how can the experient feel sure that imagination, or the natural tendency to interpret in terms of sensory phenomena, has not led him to distort a swift and surprising E S P-type impression? Another advantage of hallucinogens is that they do not arouse instinctive bias. A man whose blood would curdle at the thought of precognition will be able to read, say, Christopher Mayhew's account of how under mescalin he experienced events at 3 o'clock, which in fact took place half an hour later, and keep quite cool.

A problem yet more difficult than lack of words is, as 'Vivian' said, lack of concepts. (Experiences under hallucinogens demonstrate this too.) 'All science,' writes Sir George Thomson, 'not only its physical side . . . depends on its concepts . . . *They determine the questions to ask and so the answers we can get.*'[1]

Here perhaps is one key to the vicious circle in which research into ESP still finds itself. Lack of concepts about it leads to lack of the right questions. That means lack of satisfactory answers and testable hypotheses. And lacking them, the phenomena go ignored. But that does not mean that they do not exist.

It may also be that some extra-sensory phenomena go unnoticed because, having no concepts for them, we fail to translate them into sensory images. Sir Frederick Bartlett has said of sensory perception that 'what is presented at once stirs up in the subject some preformed bias, interest, or some persistent temperamental factors, and he at once adopts towards the situation some fairly specific attitude. . . . This is why . . . certain special features of the object always stand out as, psychologically, the most important parts of the whole presented. 'Because this factor,' he goes on, 'is always present, it is fitting to speak of . . . perceiving, imagining, remembering, thinking and reasoning as an *effort after meaning.*'[2]

When the Fuegians saw the *Beagle* they did not even notice it because in terms of their experience it had no meaning. In a recent article Dr Richard Gregory has suggested that space travellers may find themselves up against the same trouble. 'Suppose,' he says, 'that we were to meet something really odd—say a new life form—could we see it properly? The perceptual system is a computer, programmed by evolutionary experience and by our own personal experience of our world. A new kind of object requires the perceptual computer to solve a new problem with an old programme, which may be neither adequate nor appropriate. There is evidence that primitive people at first see aircraft with feathers on their wings, and the early microscopists and explorers reported weird and wonderful creatures. Both intellectually and visually we tend to see things in terms of our previous experience or fantasies, and both new objects and new ideas are difficult to

[1] My italics. Sir George Thomson, *The Inspiration of Science* (O.U.P., 1961), p. 4.
[2] Sir Frederick Bartlett, F.R.S. *Remembering* (C.U.P., 1950), p. 62.

accept or to 'see' straight. The exploration of new worlds will be hazardous not only from without, but also from within ourselves.'[3]

Perhaps, then, it is not to be wondered at if computers programmed to deal with sensory perceptions interpret extrasensory phenomena either not at all, or with weird and wonderful results which are angrily rejected by other computers who stick to their official material. To end this chapter I cannot resist summarizing a little story which illustrates the *impasse* in a nut shell. An idealistic American Minister of Religion, Dr Ralph Harlow, went for a country walk with his wife, and they jointly experienced a vivid visual hallucination of six divinely beautiful female figures. In the light of their religious beliefs they very naturally interpreted this hallucination as 'seeing angels'. Shortly afterwards Dr Harlow had to attend a Congress on Religious Education, and, although intensely embarrassed, he felt it his duty to tell his fellows clerics about his uplifting experience. But they were not at all uplifted. On the contrary they were extremely shocked, and no one asked him a single question. At last one of his colleagues broke the dreadful silence. What Dr Harlow had seen, he said, must have been a swarm of bees.[4]

[3] Richard Gregory, 'Visual Illusions in Space', *New Scientist*, August 30th, 1962.

[4] Dr S. Ralph Harlow, *Life after Death* (Gollancz, 1960).

CHAPTER XXIII

Mescalin Visions

Some people who are prone to E S P-type experiences relating to mundane events also have spontaneous experiences which resemble those induced by mescalin and other hallucinogens. For that reason it was suggested to me that my experiences under mescalin might throw some oblique light on such temperaments. At first I jibbed at this idea, for nowadays celestial visions under hallucinogens are almost a glut on the market. And I did have celestial visions. Moreover, unless one is a master of words—and even the masters do not find it too easy—to try to describe such visions is rather like trying to reproduce the *Matthew Passion* on a tin lid with a spoon.

To escape feeling self-conscious about my visions I shall not write from memory, but from a tape recording made when I was under the drug and from notes dictated before I was entirely back to normal. In that state the experient has no inhibitions about what he describes. I even forgot how embarrassing it is for a more or less sophisticated Englishwoman to talk about Love in an idealistic fashion—quite apart from the variety of phenomena covered by that elastic word.

I was given mescalin in 1952 by a doctor who was studying model psychoses in a search for a cure for schizophrenia. Mr Huxley's book, *The Doors of Perception*, had not come out, hallucinogens were not yet fashionable, and I had no idea what to expect. Though early training helped me to conceal it, I was in a blue funk.

The basic difference between my experiences and Mr Huxley's is that for him the outer world was altered and transfigured, whereas for me it became extremely drab and boring. My consciousness fled away into a stupendous inner world where years of experience passed between the utterance in the outer world of one word and the next, where time and space seemed interchangeable and where my surroundings were more ever-moving than the Bay of Biscay in a storm. This is in line with some exclamations made by Mrs Willett when she felt herself drawn into the world of her ostensible communicators. 'I'm all with things flitting past me,' she cried, and again soon afterwards, 'How *nothing* time is! All human experience is one.'[1]

That sense of oneness was the core of my experience. The doctor asked me if, when I found one thing taking the place of another, I could see the connections between the two; to which I replied contemptuously, 'It's quite simple. They are the same thing. It's seeing from the *middle*, you see.'

This difference in kind from sensory experience creates a problem. The deeper I travelled into that inner hinterland, the more vital I felt it to be exactly truthful, exactly accurate, and yet the more clumsy and misleading ordinary language became. Such words as here or there, far or near, up or down, then or now, were simply not applicable in a world where everything seemed to be in a sphere—a non-spatial one—and where objects were not only perceived from the outside but their 'becomingness' was also entered into and shared. (A reminder here, perhaps, of Gilbert Murray's description of E S P as 'feeling with'?) Another way to describe that curious state of consciousness is to say that one appeared to experience relationships; and sometimes their intensity became overwhelming. At one point I cried out in apprehension, 'If you are too caught up in all those relationships you will be exploded.' That, incidentally, is what the E S P-prone temperament also shrinks from in ordinary life, being caught up in the emotional relationships of other people.

To convey the mescalin experience, as in my sharing of 'Vivian's' condition of scope and freedom, one can only resort to analogies, similes, poetic images, and these must always be misleading since the experience, in my case, was never auditory, nor could it really be defined as visual. And yet, paradoxically, I found myself in a world of fabulous colour, a thousand times more vivid and varied than a kingfisher's feathers or tropical flowers or the Crown Jewels. The nearest I have seen to it in the outer world is the west window of Chartres cathedral with the afternoon sun shining through it. The experience of fantastic colour under hallucinogens is well known, and some people who

[1] *Proceedings*, S.P.R., Vol. XLIII.

have had ESP-type experiences about mundane matters have had it spontaneously. I did so myself for a fleeting moment when I appeared to climb out of my body up a Chopin Ballade. Under mescalin this phase culminated for me in a blinding flash of illumination, white beyond all colour, and, so it seemed at the time, spiritual as well as aesthetic. But I was soon brought back to earth by the doctor asking, 'Which were the most pleasant of the images you have just seen?'

Pleasant! What a drivelling little word to use, I thought. Every time the doctor called me back I had the same sense of diving down from real life into dirty mud that I had had as a girl when waking up from sleep. But then I could not remember what I had left. Now I could. So too could Mrs Willett when coming out of a spell of dissociation during which she appeared to visit her discarnate friends. 'It's just like waking up in prison when one has been at home,' she said. 'Don't you ever walk out of yourself? It's heavenly to be out of oneself—when I'm everything, you know, and everything else is me.'[2]

To walk out of oneself—perhaps the most splendid of all experiences. It can happen, too, in the world of sense, to children entranced by a new discovery; to workers in a group and players in a team; to artists transferring a vision to words or notes or canvas; and also to performers, musicians, actors, athletes, whenever the play, the music, the race, the game—the Other—in itself becomes all in all and one's own little self is utterly forgotten. For me under mescalin this experience was at times complete. My body vanished. My ego vanished. I lived in the things that I became aware of. That, of course, does not have to be all jam. It was quite revolting, for instance, when, as I mentioned in Chapter III, I was given the letter of a furiously indignant man to hold and felt suffocated in his disgusting dark brown anger. I had always known what sensitives meant when they said that hatred pierced them like a spear and love was a warm and shining light. Now I knew still better. (How many children are sensitive in this way? How many feel suffocated by the anger, open or repressed, of their grown ups?)

For no reason that I can discern I was passionately concerned

2 *Proceedings*, S.P.R., Vol. XLIII.

under mescalin about one problem: Did evil exist as such, or were those who sought it mistakenly seeking good in the wrong direction? However that might be, the sense of evil at times was very strong. At one grim moment I knew that I must clear out—and at once—from the brink of some Dark Centre (it seemed to be mixed up with Zimbabwe in central Africa), whence something was about to rise which I knew I should not have the strength to face. Clearing out in that mental world did not mean the clumsy trundling away of a body, but a switch of consciousness. Apparently I escaped by remembering—I quote my notes—'the square on the hypotenuse [this meant the Pythagorean theorem, but my mind was working in images, not words] and that seemed a . . . principle clean of all emotions, and in that clear yellow light I could for a moment rest. As I remembered the theorem a tremendous stylized sun rose up and the world was sheer glory.'

The glory of mathematics to a mathematician is well known, and since taking mescalin I have read of three gifted men whom a mathematical proposition lifted into a serene and perfect world. But what psychological quirk enabled a geometrical theorem to rescue a woman who was certainly no mathematician from a foreboding of evil too great to be borne?

Many people have experienced symbols of universal interrelatedness under a hallucinogen, and mystics, artists, saints and sensitives do the same on their own. To me, under mescalin, that inter-relatedness was symbolized by a delicate spidery web, like the filaments on a cactus, which linked everything to everything from atom to nebula. Not that there were solid objects or solid threads. Nothing was static. The entire Universe was in constant fluid movement. Gradually I became aware of that movement as a crucial fact: it was *The Dance,* the inter-weaving eternal impersonal relentless inevitable Cosmic Dance—the Dance of Beingness. I saw the God, Krishna, dancing—'dancing', I cried out in extreme delight, 'with pure happiness!'

Part of the Dance was an endless frieze of Hindu Deities, modulating and intertwining for ever like a fugue. They were representations, I knew, of Great Essences far beyond human conception. Then, in a flash that filled me with awe, beyond and behind them—but such words meant nothing—there appeared a supreme Figure, motionless, Buddha-like, eternally at peace. 'Now

I see,' I thought, 'why Orientals seek Nirvana.' If indeed they had developed even a dim awareness of the relentless eternal Dance, a profound longing would ensue for the ultimate still point at which all movement ceased. Pondering later on this experience brought home to me the evocative power of art. When young I had been to the Rodin Exhibition at the Victoria and Albert Museum. At the end of the hall where his fluid rhythmic sculptures were set out sat a towering Buddha, who gazed down on them from a great height, in remote and passionless calm. At that time I could not formulate what moved me so deeply at the juxtaposition of the Buddha and the Rodins. Now I seemed to have found out what it was. The artists had bodied forth hints of the two great opposites, stillness and movement, on which the life of the universe depends.

Once more the doctor brought me back with a bump to earth by what seemed an utterly futile request to tell him when I thought a quarter of a minute had passed. I did this twice—correctly—with the sour comment that during his quarter of a minute I had had time to travel the equivalent of several times round the world. 'And when you blink,' I added inconsequently, 'it is like a whole mountain range.'

This surprised him, for at that moment something had made him blink with unusual vigour. Yet he had blindfolded me and in any case I kept my eyes tightly closed to shut out the dreary boring outer world. Had I made the remark by chance, then, or was it telepathic, or even due to some unknown method of becoming aware of physical objects? If so, could this suggest that the impression of an invisible man, which my two friends and I had felt in the little back room at the S.P.R., was due to our subconscious contact with Carington's records which were stored there behind a curtain?

The religiously gifted have always held that to develop E S P for its own sake and irrespective of the stability of the experient is to ask for trouble. My mescalin experiences certainly confirmed this for me. To travel far into the hinterland of consciousness unprepared is about as overwhelming as to round the Straits of Magellan in a boat designed for a nice afternoon on the Thames. A point came at last when the relentless splendour of the Cosmic Dance, perceived, not through a glass darkly, but face to face, became quite simply too much. I felt that in another second I should be disintegrated by sheer excess of glory. 'Human kind cannot bear too much reality.' And then, just at cracking point, it dawned on me that with all that Cosmic Perfection, there was still something lacking. Everything, everywhere, was clearly inter-related in that vast Unity. But—it did not know it! The Universe did not know that it was one. At that staggering discovery I some-how pulled myself together and fumblingly, quiveringly, asked a question: 'Is there no conscious communication in all this inter-weaving Unity? Where is Love?'

There are fairy stories where the hero utters a magic word and the impossible happens. Mircea Eliade points out somewhere that when, on a higher level, Parsifal asked, 'Where is the Grail?' at his question all life was renewed. The question, 'Where is Love?' was my magic word, and the answer it evoked was such that even now, ten years later and, so experts assure me, officially sane, it seems idiotic on my part to try to describe it. One thing at least is fortunate, that transcendent experiences under hallu-cinogens have become so frequent that I shall not be accused of believing that I was favoured with a special revelation. It was rather that the sun shines on the just and the unjust alike. At the same time, I did really ask a question—one so seldom does—and it has, after all, been said by no small authority that those who ask receive.

To try to describe the answer I will quote from my notes dic-tated while still partially under the drug. Though childish and incoherent they are at least not self-conscious or furbished up. 'Out of the gold,' I said, 'there appeared a figure clothed in soft blues and greens and purples, infinitely benign and compassionate. I knew it to be the Divine Mother and her symbols were in a sense not diamonds but pearls. She was like a pearl coming into a world of diamond.'

'The gold' stood for a world of pure spirit—in the sense of spiri-tuality, nothing to do with discarnate spirits. It is a pity that the word has the double meaning. I recognized this world as beyond and apart from form, and one I could no more enter than a gnat could fly into the sun. It seemed important never to be so daz-zled by the beauty of any form as to equate it, as such, with spirit.

Spirit could shine through forms, however humble, but to equate the two would be idolatry.

It appeared to be the fact that I asked the magic question which enabled the Divine Mother to come, a messenger from the Centre, to answer it. And her answer was—I wish I knew what words to use—to swing me round into alignment with her, so that I could look, not towards her, but with a fraction of her eyes outward on all created things. In this way she gave me a glimpse of what Love was: infinitely far from possessive doting, quite unsentimental, yet warm and comforting—and, above all, personal. That was the wonderful thing about it; no nonsense here about cold impersonal benevolence. Most people know what it is to be in love with a single human being before the desire to be loved in return obtrudes and when it is pure delight to serve that being, whether he or she knows it or not. That was the Divine Mother's attitude to all and everything. She was literally in love with the whole Universe. What entranced me was that this resulted, not in soulful uplift or juicy sentiment, but in gaiety, a gaiety far beyond the reach of any scherzo or even of wind-blown daffodils or sunlit seas. Soon after she came, some children began to shout and sing in the street outside, and since mescalin can induce hypersensitivity to sound, the doctor asked me if I minded them. Mind a child singing! It was as if she allowed me to share her divine amusement at such a deliciously silly idea.

The sense of alignment with the Divine Mother again stimulated the desire I had caught from the doctor to help the mentally sick, and made me say to him, 'What exactly are you trying to find out through me?'

'What goes on in the mind of a schizophrenic,' he replied.

I doubt if in those days I had any knowledge of the schizophrenic's withdrawal from life or of the tragic suspicion he can develop of other men, though I may have read and subsequently forgotten some article about it, rarely as such topics were mentioned in the public press at the time. However that may be, I now felt that my job was to go and explore the terrible side of the schizophrenic's world. I did this consciously. And terrible it was. At its furthest point I came on a cold, grey, stony, El Greco-like desert, its monotony broken only by jagged rocks. There was not a leaf to be seen anywhere, not a blade of grass. Huddled far apart among the rocks were grey veiled figures, motionless, unable to communicate, 'at the bottom', beyond despair. They were, I knew, the Lost. I have never before or since felt the total compassion I felt then. I remember pausing by one of them and thinking desperately, 'Is there nothing I can do to rouse and comfort him?'

And the answer was—nothing. I could make no contact. I was not good enough. None less, it appeared, than the perfectly Good could help the Lost, and to do so they had to sink in sacrifice, even below them, to become the objects of their pity and compassion. It was only by giving those at the bottom a chance to help others who needed it that they could be saved. And by some strange paradox only the perfectly Good could get below them to need their love.

My 'sane' attitude to this part of my model psychosis is curious. I had previously disliked the word sacrifice, I suspect because it was mixed up with the presentation of Christianity that I had fled from in my youth. And now, intellectually, the paradox of the Good and the Lost seems to make little sense. But I cannot wriggle out of the conviction that it is a feeble effort to express some hidden truth.

I did not drop at once from the exalted sense of alignment with the Divine Mother to my usual more or less Pink Me level. Two days after my official return to sanity I was cooking the lunch, pondering my experiences and thinking how wonderful it would be if all human beings would only realize that they were in actual fact members of one another. As I pondered I had a throw-back. The Divine Mother came again, in no way visually, but in the immediate interior fashion that the ostensible Julia and Vivian had done. At the time, what she then intimated seemed the highest sense and as practical as the remark that to put sugar in your tea would make it sweeter. I must confess that it still does. But I have little doubt that any attempt to reproduce it in words for other people will sound like sentimental nonsense. It was quite simple—that the Universe could not become conscious of its unity until the principle of communication, which was the kind of love she had made me aware of, had been injected into it. To do that was the next task. . . .

At her coming I fell into a state of total calm and happiness and lack of desire. But not lack of energy. Even cooking the lunch—I loathe cooking—became an ecstatic act of service. I can only describe the feeling as a kind of integration, a complete lack of conflict. I was unified. But of course the mood did not last. How could it? It had not been earned. Still, I do remember it, though I cannot recapture its intensity, and I know quite well that it would be my highest good to recover it. In fact, I owe a great deal to my model psychosis. For a moment it tweaked my eyes open. Now at least I know that they are shut, that my senses are merely parochial and that to take my yapping little ego at all seriously is quite ridiculous. And part of me knows too—though that part is often asleep—that, whatever intellect may say to the contrary, somewhere, somehow, the Centre does exist.

The comments made by experts who were professionally interested in my model psychosis were diverse and entertaining. A Freudian summed it up with easy confidence. 'It's obvious,' he said, 'Your Divine Mother was a construct of your own. You were doubtless brought up in an Edwardian nursery and saw too little of your own mother.'

True, perhaps, but I had no doubt my mother loved me, and as for my being able to create that celestial figure, I could as well believe myself capable of knocking off the works of Shakespeare and Beethoven in my sleep. A Jungian analyst looked delighted. 'An archetype!' he exclaimed. A Catholic said reverently, 'Our Lady!' Another psychiatrist called the whole experience entirely negative, and yet another pronounced Mrs Heywood's Divine Mother to be Mrs Heywood herself. That enraged me at first. Then, suddenly, I saw that it was very funny.

What label the experts choose to give this product of my model psychosis seems of no importance at all. They can say she was due to artificial over-stimulation of the parasympathetic nervous system if they like. What matters to the experient is that in the sense that I know the Madonna of the Rocks to be a better picture than the Monarch of the Glen, *Deh Vieni* a better song than *Lili Marlene* and Abraham Lincoln a finer character than Hitler, I know that, whatever she was, she represented all that I could possibly grasp of perfection. This has nothing to do with dogma, the survival of death, or intellectual formulation of any kind. It is merely a matter of recognizing Quality when one sees it.

CHAPTER XXIV

Back to Earth

I once remarked to a shrewd American business man that I thought telepathy was an established fact. To which he replied with a laugh. 'So what? Does it matter at all if one unimportant person occasionally picks up an unimportant fact about another unimportant person? Now, if you could use it instead of the telephone. . . .'

True, perhaps. But what of its implications? If such 'picking-up' can throw an unsuspected light both on our relations to those twin mysteries called time and space and to each other, if E S P is a hidden means of communication between man and man—and, so some incidents suggest, between man and animal—then we had better know it, even though its practical use on the conscious level may be a mirage, or at least far over the horizon.

But how are we to come to know it? Research into E S P is at present a Cinderella; it brings neither profit nor prestige. Nor, as yet, is there any accepted body of principles or techniques on which to base it. Experimenters still have to work on a trial and error basis—they do not even know what the variables are, much less how to control them—and the few contemporary philosophers who have the courage to envisage E S P can do little more than speculate about it in the dark. Were things otherwise it would be silly to imagine that a record of trivial E S P-type experiences—E S P-*type* only, since from the evidential point of view they need not be due to E S P at all—might contribute to research by suggesting factors which could help or hamper it. But the situation being what it is, anything seems worth trying, especially as my experiences are so far from unique. Hundreds of other ordinary people have similar experiences in comparable circumstances, and the views of those I have talked to about the factors which seem to affect them are usually much the same as mine. For that reason it may be worth trying to summarize what these are.

I am only too well aware that my own views are coloured by the conviction which my experiences eventually forced on me, that there exists permanent subconscious communication between other people and myself, in proportion to my affection for them and possibly to theirs for me, or to the desire in one of us for help which the other could give. If that is true for me, it is surely true for everyone, though the closeness of the hidden linkage may vary according to temperament. But to be linked means to affect and to be affected. Beneath the surface, then, we may all be directly affecting each other all the time.

Professor H. H. Price has suggested a further rather unnerving possibility: that ideas as such—any of the ideas we have ever had—including mental images, may have a tendency to persist independently of their authors. Moreover, once having escaped those authors, so to speak, he thinks that they may have a tendency to express themselves somehow, through some consciousness, somewhere. But there is one consolation: he feels that conflicting ideas probably tend to cancel each other out. If any of this speculation be well-founded, what a man thinks and feels and imagines may count for as much as what he does; when cogitating alone in his bath he may be as potent for good or ill as when haranguing a crowd.[1]

The hypothesis of subconscious interlinkage is an additional help in explaining the one thing about E S P which at least is certain and which must affect our efforts to track it down: that is its tendency to arouse in many people, including researchers, either a violent desire to prove that it exists or an equally violent one to prove that it does not.

It is worth considering these attitudes a little further. In addition to the obvious motives which make some people pro-E S P there may also be an unrecognized longing to bring up to consciousness the knowledge of subconscious interlinkage, to convince the isolated surface mind that one is not alone. Researchers would feel as well a natural desire for their work to produce positive results—and results which conformed to their hopes. Total impartiality is a lot to ask, especially where one's own kind is involved. 'As soon as I discovered anything which had not been discovered before,' said Swedenborg of his own researches into anatomy, 'I began—seduced probably by self-love—to grow blind

[1] *Proceedings*, S.P.R., Vol. L, p. 1 et seq.

to the most acute . . . researches of others. . . . Nay, when I tried to form principles from these [his own] discoveries I thought I could detect much to confirm their truth in various other phenomena, although in reality they were fairly susceptible of no construction of the kind.'[2] And Professor R. A. Fisher has pointed out that even some of Mendel's findings were biassed in the direction he wanted and that each generation since Mendel seems to have found in his papers what it wished to find and ignored the rest. These are warnings that experients as well as researchers can profitably bear in mind.

The desire to reject E S P, on the other hand, may be due in part to the opposite attitude, to fear of subconsciously realized interlinkage in those people who have a strong desire for privacy and independence and are determined to defend their precious personal identity at any price. Such a fear might perhaps be enough to prevent their conscious minds from accepting E S P, whatever the evidence for it. In Chapter I, I mentioned a number of other powerful reasons for its rejection, but they do not entirely account for the curious fact that some people who expend much time and energy in the search for it sometimes appear to give away by what look like Freudian slips that the one thing they apparently do not want is to find it.

Such feebly corroborated experiences as mine are easy game for people who fear E S P. 'Drunkards experience pink elephants,' is about all they need say, and it sounds reasonable enough. But their arguments against the experimental evidence for it are not unlike those given by Dr Johnson to illustrate how simple it is to support one's denial of something ones does not like with a splendid show of reason.[3]

[2] Signe Toksvig, *Swedenborg* (Faber, 1949), p. 3.
[3] 'I deny that Canada is taken and I can support my denial with pretty good arguments. The French are a much more numerous people than we; it is not likely that they would allow us to take it. "But the Ministry tell us so."—True. But the Ministry have put us to an enormous expense and it is to their interest to persuade us that we have got something for our money. "But we are told so by thousands of men who were at the taking of it."—Ay, but these men have still more interest in deceiving us. They don't want you should think they have gone on a fool's errand; and they don't want you should think that the French have beat them, but that they beat the French. Now suppose you should go over and see if it is so, that would only satisfy yourself; for when you come home we will not believe you. We will say you

To what extent does emotional dislike of E S P, even in the general public, hamper inquiry into it? Hostility must obviously hamper any inquiry, but hostility to the idea that the earth went round the sun did not prevent its doing so. Here, on the contrary, if E S P *is* E S P and does imply subconscious inter-communication, hostility may actually inhibit its appearance, especially if, as Professor Price suggests, an idea can cancel out its opposite. That, he says, may be one reason why nowadays telepathy is a comparatively rare occurrence, because of mutual inhibitions. 'It is also a reason why it may fail to occur if there are sceptical spectators. Indeed the sceptics need not even be spectators. It will be enough if the general climate of opinion is sceptical. . . . In an age of faith, when the general climate of opinion is credulous instead of sceptical, it is presumably the other way round.'[4]

Is there here, then, a splendid joke on the part of Nature, that some degree of unscientific bias in favour of E S P may be an advantage, or even a necessity, if it is to be coaxed to appear in conditions which will put it on the map of science as definitely, for instance, as a magnetic field?

There is another way in which Western man's strong sense of separate identity may inhibit the emergence of E S P. The more separate one person feels from another—in other words the less affection he feels for him—the more of himself he automatically wants to hide. The very young and the very primitive seem to hide little or nothing, and anecdotes hint that they exercise E S P more readily than sophisticated Western adults. There are some exceptions though, such as Socrates, perhaps, and Swedenborg and Gilbert Murray, all men, incidentally, with an unusually strong sense of kinship with their fellows. Anecdotes about less exceptional lives also hint that the more concern one person feels for another, the more likely is spontaneous telepathy to be observed between them. A typical example is the disturbing dream which repeatedly worried the father of Joan of Arc, that his young

---

have been bribed.'—Quoted by Boswell in his *London Journal* (Heinemann, 1950), p. 301.

I am indebted to Mr Basil Smith for drawing my attention to the delightful aptness of this passage in relation to the situation *vis-à-vis* E S P to-day.

[4] From a lecture published in *Proceedings*, S.P.R., Vol. L.

daughter was about to go away from home with some soldiers. This was long before she had mentioned her project of joining the Dauphin in order to save France, but after she had begun to receive instruction from her Voices to do so—and her mind, in consequence, was full of the idea.

Over and above the general factors which affect our chances of learning more about E S P, there are also the immediate problems of experimental research into it. Right away this runs into an *impasse*: that the standards and methods of the physical sciences demand evidence repeatable to order, and that E S P cannot be invoked to order. So far, the only way out has been to confine experiment to such monotonous tasks as guessing the order of distant cards or drawings, in numbers large enough for the significance of the scores to be assessed by statistical methods. Invaluable as this work has been, it has certain limitations. High scores may be evidence of the existence of E S P, but they give the minimum of information about the process. So far from conscious is the 'guessing' that the 'guesser' does not even know when he has made a hit. Nevertheless, experimentation has turned up some clues, among them that a particular 'guesser' can make significant scores with one agent and not with another; that a receptive attitude to the idea that the experiment is capable of demonstrating E S P leads to higher scores than disbelief; and—a nice observation this—that on occasion people hostile to E S P have scored significantly below chance level, thus hinting that subconsciously they knew the right card, but did not intend to take part in establishing the authenticity of so irrational a phenomenon.

How, then, are more revealing examples of E S P to be evoked in experimental conditions? This is a question to which any of us any day might stumble on an answer. But it is not an easy one. To this experient, E S P-type impressions seem to divide, roughly, into two kinds. The first is reaction to the immediate environment, which very occasionally passes over into a 'going out' from the ego- and humanity-centred self to participate for a moment in a greater unity. My experiences on Dartmoor and in Westminster Hall were minor examples of this kind of thing, and so was my sense of alignment with the Divine Mother when 'out of my mind' under mescalin. But it is hard to see any experimental pattern into which such experiences could be forced, and it is reasonable enough for people who have not had them to label them mere fantasy.

The second kind of impression is mainly inter-human and is usually a response to a person, a problem, a minor irritation, a crisis—all forms of stimulus which could, in theory, be produced to order. Even so, spontaneous E S P-type experiences still suggest that to get positive results a whole string of factors need to be favourable at the right moment. The most tricky problem seems to be evasion of the censor, that threshold of consciousness whose main function, according to Bergson and Professor H. H. Price, is to exclude any image which does not serve a man's immediate interests at the time. One talented experient put it that before trying to exercise E S P she had to get her conscious self out of the way. Unfortunately most of the few who can do this deliberately dislike making the attempt except in an ultra-sympathetic atmosphere and for a reason that seems to them valid; and the proof or analysis of E S P itself is anything but such a reason. Worse, most of them are bored to tears by the monotony of repeatedly guessing uninteresting symbols—and what better way than boredom to reduce emotional fuel? Boredom, it is true, has occasionally been counter-balanced by affection for the experimenter, or the desire to shine, or even to make money, but, in general, to ask a person who has a tendency to E S P-type experience to try to exercise E S P at a given moment, under inspection, is about as inhibiting as to ask a poet to write a masterpiece in a crowd between the hours of ten and ten-fifteen. One such person said to me, 'The very idea of doing those experiments ties my middle into a knot.'

I have sometimes wondered whether my sojourn in the mescalin world provided a clue to that somewhat exaggerated revulsion. It is extremely hard to put into words, and the best one can say is that perceptions in that world were of fluid relationships rather than of static objects, and as a result, values were different. If E S P is an upwelling from a part of the psyche which normally perceives the world in such a fashion, the experient's interest would tend to lie in relationships themselves rather than in what one friend of mine called 'the perturbations of time and space that they might cause'. The order of a pack of cards would seem to him an isolated secondary phenomenon, interlinking with nothing, leading nowhere beyond itself. It would be the equivalent of the separated chemical components of a hyacinth, to an artist who wanted to paint the living flower.

In telepathic experiments factors affecting the agent as well as the experient also come into the picture. Spontaneous experiences suggest that both his situation at the time and the basic relationship between the two can affect results. In some successful guessing experiments, it is true that relationship has been no more than an unknown kind of compatibility between mere acquaintances; but if emotional fuel is an element which aids telepathy, that fuel might be induced more easily if, say, husband and wife, parent and child, teacher and pupil, or twins, or lovers, were to act as subjects. As against this, repeatedly to induce emotional fuel in close relationships might cause trouble. Nor would it be easy to do in experimental conditions.

What it all seems to come to, paradoxically, is that the more fundamental E S P turns out to be as a factor in relationships within, and possibly beyond, humanity, the more difficult will be its pursuit in experimental conditions until we know more about how it works. Are we then back to where we started? Is the field study of E S P-type experiences still worth while, on the chance that some of them may be genuine E S P and may provide some clues as to how to tackle it systematically? After all, field work does not preclude strict experimentation. But it has its own problems. Most people, for instance, report single experiences or at the most two or three. If asked to watch for more, their conscious attention gets turned on the job and this discourages E S P. Who has ever heard of an apparition consenting to appear when a group of would-be observers sits up to wait for it? There are also people who revel in being the centre of attention, and in order to hang on to that agreeable position serve up the vaguest coincidences as triumphs of E S P. Others, again, specialize in allegedly precognitive warnings, which are pretty obviously induced by their own fears, and are not fulfilled. An investigator out in the field needs to be equipped with many buckets, if not of cold, at least of tepid water, though he must also be ready to encourage the diffident people who lack the courage to confess to apparently irrational experiences.

The most tricky problem of all, however, is to know when to pour cold water on oneself. Is it worse to dismiss an experience as a chance coincidence when it may be E S P and could teach one something, or to take it as E S P when it is not? Many incidents fall into this puzzling category. Here are three to which I have no idea of the right answer. If forced to guess I should have to toss a coin.

In 1938 I was taken to Rotterdam to see the magnificent newly-discovered Vermeer. It had been hung reverently in a room by itself and was very fine, but as I looked at it the word, 'New, new, new . . .' kept echoing through my mind. I lacked the courage to say this, and even told myself that the impression was due to the picture having been cleaned. But was it? For the picture was new, being one of van Meegeren's splendid fakes.

Years later, after the war, I was less cowardly. A friend took me to an exhibition of ultra-modern art at the gallery of a famous dealer. The dealer was a majestic figure in a beard and a Russian blouse, and he showed us round, very solemnly, in person, and at the end asked for our comments in his visitors' book. My reply appalled me. It was, 'Very well, but I must put what I think, that every picture in the place is detestable and not one of them is real.'

I could have sunk into the ground with shame, but the dealer roared with laughter, 'You're right,' he said, 'I've put on the show as a hoax and you're the first person to see it.'

But how did I see it? I am no expert on modern art, for which I care very little. Did I then exercise better judgment than many experts? It seems to me less improbable that I picked up telepathically the dealer's hidden amusement as he waited for us to make fools of ourselves by writing words of praise. But I cannot be sure.

My last example is less trivial and more complex. One day in the autumn of 1962, as we were finishing luncheon, my husband handed me a £5 note, saying, 'You haven't bought yourself anything for ages. Go out and get a nice jumper.'

This astounded me, for he knows I always buy what I need, but never, especially at my age, like that 'for fun'. Still, I thought, it would be lovely to indulge in such madness, just for once. But not that afternoon. I was too busy. However, later on in the afternoon I felt that after all I must go down to Peter Jones right away and get a jumper. This was a bore, but I did go and was turning over a pile of delectable garments when equally forcibly came the impression, 'This is all nonsense. You don't want a jumper. Go home now.'

Feeling rather sour at a stupidly wasted afternoon I set off home, and half-way there, clinging pitifully to the railings, I came on a huddled quivering man. Tears were pouring down his cheeks and he was clearly at the end of his tether. 'Can I help?' I asked.

'I'm desperate,' he muttered and half turned round. Then I saw that he had had polio and that it was no good taking him home with me as I should not be able to get him up our steep stairs. 'Come into the Royal Court Hotel and we'll have a cup of tea,' I said. 'And then you can tell me your trouble.'

'If I ate or drank now,' he said, 'I should be sick.' Then, with a little persuasion, he told me. He had recently been discharged from hospital after polio, and the only room he could afford to rent was on the top floor of a hostel where they provided no food. It took him over an hour to crawl up and down the stairs. After a long and weary search he had that morning found a ground floor room which he could afford, but because the landlady had been let down by the previous tenant she was afraid to risk not having the rent in advance. And he had not got it. He had just been to see the mother of another polio victim, because she had been kind to him and had had him to tea, and he felt sure that she would lend him the money. But she had gone away for a week. 'And I can't,' he added, 'I simply can't go on dragging my body up and down those stairs any longer!'

'There you are,' said Orders smugly, as if they had timed the whole affair to a second. So I obediently fished out my £5 note and at least had the satisfaction of seeing that little bit of paper switch despair into a vision of the heavens opening.

But what is the experient to think? Ought I to look on such a string of coincidences—my husband's unusual gift, my own inconsequent impulses, the apt meeting—as an inner pattern of communication, of relationship, a kind of inner *Gestalt*, or as just a random series of chance happenings, 'a little bit of luck' for the poor victim? If I had not seen my son look up a street in a map because he was shortly to be asked where it was by a stranger, I might plump for the latter. And suppose I were wrong. Would I thereby reduce the capacity for response on similar occasions?

Research then into the process of ESP is as complicated as a detective story: complicated by the general mental climate, by personal relationships, by problems of timing and emergence. For that reason the more intriguing. That it has not as yet got very far need not be a discouragement. After all, the subject has only been tackled for eighty odd years, and at that largely by volunteers with their own money in their own time—and in a general atmosphere of disapproval.[5] Compare this with the astronomical expenditure of time, skill and money on missile research, or even on checking Einstein's theory that the force of gravity can deflect light. One day, perhaps, ESP will get its own Einstein who with some inspired generalization will make this jumble of apparently irrational phenomena fall into a meaningful pattern. And then, as Sir Julian Huxley has said, its untapped possibilities may prove to be as important and extraordinary as the once unsuspected electrical possibilities of matter.

They could also prove just as dangerous. If ESP exists, if it underlies all our overt relationships, if it has these vast untapped possibilities, the sooner we know it the better. That does not mean it would be a good thing for all and sundry to know how to exercise it at will. How many of us, at the present stage of our evolution, could be trusted with the power to probe into the secrets of another man's heart—and even to modify his thinking—

[5] Disapproval seems to be waning in unexpected quarters. A Czech psychologist, Dr Milan Rýzl, has recently reported some remarkable evidence for telepathy produced by a hypnotized subject under controlled conditions. And in 1962 the Professor of Physiology at Leningrad University, L. L. Vasiliev, brought out two books reporting successful experiments in ESP done by himself and others. One of these books, *Long Distance Suggestion* (Moscow, Gospolitizdat) begins by quoting a remark by a Russian scientist, K. E. Ciolkovsky, who is well known in the USSR as a rocket flight pioneer. 'The phenomena of telepathy,' he says, 'can no longer be called into question. . . . We must highly esteem the attempt at elucidating them in the light of science.' Since this book went to press Professor Vasiliev's other book on ESP, *Mental Suggestion*, has appeared in English (Galley Hill Press, Church Crookham, Hants.). It records several series of experiments in which, he says, hypnotized subjects were successfully sent to sleep and awakened at a distance, at will. On occasion both agent and subject were placed in metal cages designed to obstruct the type of electromagnetic wave which he and his colleagues had previously assumed to convey the signal. The subject's responses he says were not affected.

and not make use of that power for selfish ends? There may be a lot to be said for the traditional mystical ban on E S P for its own sake.

However, danger from excess of conscious E S P is scarcely imminent, if only because it seems to carry the built-in safeguard that concern for others is the most favourable condition for its emergence. Meanwhile, we of the rank and file can amuse ourselves by keeping an eye on our own reactions, if or when we come across an apparent spontaneous example of it. What would that be for us? A revelation from on high, something nasty in the woodshed, pure imagination, or a natural phenomenon not necessarily separated by any hard and fast line from those our senses allow us to look on as respectable?

And what, too, would our reactions to it tell us about ourselves? That we feel safer living in splendid isolation, à huis clos? Or that we are prepared to face the possibility of being members of one another in a world which, as mathematicians already know, is first and foremost one of relationships, and which now, as a great mathematician, Hermann Weyl, has dramatically put it, is being made by modern science itself 'to appear more and more as an open one . . . pointing beyond itself.'[6]

[6] Quoted by A. S. Eddington in a foreword to A. A. Brockington's *Mysticism and Poetry* (Chapman and Hall, 1934).